"Psalm-praying is one of the oldest and most powerful ways of learning to talk to God. Yet the words of the Psalms are distant from us, and Christians are not always sure how to make those ancient words *our* words. Smith and Wilt provide in this book the kindling for our own Psalm-praying, provoking our response and forming the word of God in our mouths. Pray the words of Scripture and then let their words spark your imagination and slow you down enough to learn the grammar of intimacy with God."

—**Glenn Packiam**, associate senior pastor, New Life Church; author of *The Resilient Pastor* and *Blessed Broken Given*

"The Psalms have been the headwaters of great English poetry and prayer since they first began to be translated, molding poets from Sir Philip Sidney, George Herbert, and Gerard Manley Hopkins all the way down to Johnny Cash and Bono. The Psalms get down into the mud of sorrow and lift the broken up into hope and joy, which is why they birthed gospel music and the blues. They will always inspire, and they will never be used up. *Sheltering Mercy* is yet another faithful child of the Psalms, a beautiful collection of poems arriving at a dark moment, poems unafraid of sorrow and brokenness, delivering hope and joy."

—**N. D. Wilson**, author of *Notes from the Tilt-a-Whirl* and *Death by Living*

"These exquisite Psalms-inspired prayers give language to my emotions at a time in history when I often find myself at a loss for words. Thank you, Ryan and Dan, for such an incredibly poetic resource!"

—**JJ Heller**, singer-songwriter

"Reading the Psalms is a very good thing to do. Singing the Psalms is even better. But best of all is when we pray the Psalms. For millennia believers have used the Psalms as a school of prayer, as a model for prayer, and as a springboard to prayer. This beautifully crafted rendering of the Psalms gives voice to the cries of our hearts, depth to our intercessions, and breadth to our supplications. Find here refreshment and renewal."

—**George Grant**, Parish Presbyterian Church, Franklin, Tennessee; author of *The Blood of the Moon* and *The Micah Mandate*

"A targum is the ancient practice of rewriting sacred text in today's vocabulary. Smith and Wilt creatively apply this historic art form to the Psalms for the purpose of renewing these ancestral cries in every human heart."

—**AJ Sherrill**, author of *Being with God* and *The Enneagram for Spiritual Formation*

"Praying the Psalms is de facto praying in technicolor. Smith and Wilt's Psalm-based book of prayers, *Sheltering Mercy*, enables us to pray them in 3D. The anchoring of these prayers in the text of the Psalms, the authors' rich offering of cross-references to other books in the Hebrew Scriptures, and culminating themes in the New Testament, plus references to treasured Christian spiritual classics content, make this volume an invaluable devotional asset."

—**Darrell A. Harris**, The Robert E. Webber Institute
for Worship Studies (emeritus)

"*Sheltering Mercy* reads like inspired literature from a friend who is speaking directly to me and my situation. It is filled with a hopefulness that creates a safe space for reflection, one that is so necessary for leaders today."

—**Eldon Fry**, spiritual director, pastoral counselor, educator, and author
of *Growing Up Idaho* and *Spiritual Formation: Attention Along the Way*

"For centuries Christians have repeated the Psalms, not only as prayer but as a school for prayer. In them we learn the patterns of praise, thanksgiving, and lament. In these eloquent meditations and improvisations on the Psalms, Smith and Wilt further that education. We are offered a guide to how these ancient songs can become more fully our own and more explicitly connected to the rest of Scripture."

—**Steven R. Guthrie**, Belmont University

"This beautiful collection of psalms expressed as poetic prayer reminds us of the relevance of reverence in our daily lives and the hope breathed through even the darkest of sufferings. Alight on a different poem each day, and find rest in its cadence, restoration in its celebration, and guidance from new songs grown from deep-rooted wisdom."

—**Carolyn Weber**, author of *Surprised by Oxford* and *Holy Is the Day*

"Over the course of my career, I've spent countless hours laboring over vocal harmonies. There's something beautiful about hearing different, complementary (or consonant) notes at the same time. The prayers in *Sheltering Mercy* produce a similar result. They harmonize with the text of Scripture and make it come alive in a whole new way."

—**Michael W. Smith**, singer-songwriter

SHELTERING MERCY

PRAYERS INSPIRED BY THE PSALMS

RYAN WHITAKER SMITH
AND DAN WILT

BrazosPress

a division of Baker Publishing Group
Grand Rapids, Michigan

For all fellow sojourners,
pilgrims, and exiles.
May your heart swell with
the hope of New Creation.

© 2022 by Ryan Whitaker Smith and Daniel L. Wilt
Illustrations © Nathan Swann

Published by Brazos Press
a division of Baker Publishing Group
PO Box 6287, Grand Rapids, MI 49516-6287
www.brazospress.com

Printed in the United States of America

All rights reserved. No part of this publication may be reproduced, stored in a retrieval system, or transmitted in any form or by any means—for example, electronic, photocopy, recording—without the prior written permission of the publisher. The only exception is brief quotations in printed reviews.

Library of Congress Cataloging-in-Publication Data
Names: Smith, Ryan Whitaker, 1983– author. | Wilt, Dan, author.
Title: Sheltering mercy : prayers inspired by the Psalms / Ryan
    Whitaker Smith and Dan Wilt.
Description: Grand Rapids, Michigan : Brazos Press, a division of
    Baker Publishing Group, [2022]
Identifiers: LCCN 2021033218 | ISBN 9781587435461 (cloth) | ISBN
    9781493435326 (pdf) | ISBN 9781493435319 (ebook)
Subjects: LCSH: Bible. Psalms, I-LXXV—Devotional use. | Prayers.
Classification: LCC BS1430.54 .S58 2022 | DDC 242/.5—dc23
LC record available at https://lccn.loc.gov/2021033218

Baker Publishing Group publications use paper produced from sustainable forestry practices and post-consumer waste whenever possible.

22   23   24   25   26   27   28   7   6   5   4   3   2

✺ CONTENTS ✺

✳ INTRODUCTION ✳

In his book *Reflections on the Psalms*, C. S. Lewis makes a simple but profound observation about praise. He notes that "the humblest, and at the same time most balanced and capacious minds" praise most, "while the cranks, misfits, and malcontents praise least."[1] In other words, the humble (or, to use the common parlance of the Psalms, *righteous*) find occasion for praise even in the worst of circumstances, while the cranks (or *wicked*) are notoriously silent when it comes to thanks—even as their riches increase and their victories abound.

To be sure, the Psalms are chiefly concerned with the subject of praise. The ornamentation of many churches today attests to this fact, and rightly so. But praise, according to the psalmists, is a more complicated matter than our modern Christian use of the term might suggest. For every comforting turn of phrase fit for a hand-painted wood plank or colorful banner, there are dozens more one would do best not to mention in the company of children.

1. C. S. Lewis, *Reflections on the Psalms* (San Francisco: HarperCollins, 2017), 109–10.

Yes, the praise we find in the Psalms is often joyful. Exuberant. A tune fit for dancing. But there is praise of another sort—the praise of the forgotten. The destitute. The fearful. The guilty. For these, praise often looks like utter desperation. Immobilizing panic. Fury. Trembling lips and a stuttering heart. The Psalms pull no punches. They remind us that worship is not only celebratory, but often mournful—the cry of those so overcome with grief, so lost in darkness, that the world of light and laughter and sun and sky seems like a half-forgotten memory. The God we serve—the One who is relentlessly present with us, even when He seems as distant as the peace we long for—is with us both in triumphant victory and in crushing defeat. In consolation and in desolation. In darkness and in light. In weeping and in rejoicing. In death and in life.

The Psalms cover the wide gamut of human experience and human emotion. They are refreshingly honest. Tactlessly blunt. They move us. Shock us. Invite us to join them in their joy and in their lament. For God is present in it *all*.

The Psalms have been used as prayers by the faithful for a few thousand years. Excellent translations are available, as well as paraphrases, commentaries, and additional resources for those wishing to study the Psalms. So what exactly are we attempting to add here?

The first prayers written for this book emerged organically from times of private devotion as an attempt to engage thoughtfully and creatively with the text—*prayerful responses*, mirroring each psalm in its tone and content. The idea was birthed from friendship—years of walking together as fellow disciples of Jesus through the ebbs and flows of life and bearing one another's burdens in prayer.

We are vocational writers in different fields—Ryan Whitaker Smith in the sphere of filmmaking and storytelling, and Dan Wilt in the world of teaching, worship, and spiritual formation. We share in common not just an abiding belief in the power of prayer, but a love for language and the cadence and musicality of lyrical poetry.

In December of 2019, we shared a small booklet with friends and family that contained twenty psalm-inspired prayers. The enthusiastic responses we received confirmed that we might, in fact, be on to something. So we continued writing.

The prayers contained in this book (covering the first seventy-five psalms) are the fruit of our labors. They are not translations or paraphrases. Neither of us pretend to be qualified for such a task. Rather, they are *responses*—prayerful, poetic sketches—written in *harmony* with Scripture. We've taken to calling them *free-verse renderings*, which is just another way of saying they are impressionistic poetry without the limitations of meter or rhyme.

Imagine a painter roaming the countryside who, stumbling upon a hidden valley, scrambles for her canvas and paints in an attempt to capture the vista before her: the rocky hillsides spilling down into a meadow of green and violet, the sun straining through the clouds to scatter its golden light across the scene. The painting that results is not the valley itself, but an *impression* of it—an attempt (however feebly) to harmonize with its beauty. We have attempted to do something like that here. The psalms are holy ground, and these prayers are lyrical paintings of what we have seen, heard, and felt while sojourning there.

Each prayer adheres to the general movement of the psalm it references, while not being constrained by it. As a result, one phrase in the original text might inspire several lines of prayerful response. We allowed ourselves the freedom to follow where the text was leading us on a personal level as we prayed along with it, and to rejoice (and frequently wrestle with) what we found there.

We have included Scripture references wherever possible. One of the unexpected joys of this endeavor was finding that the whole body of Scripture was providing content for these prayers. Which brings us to another important point: as followers of Jesus, we felt the freedom to approach these prayers through the lens of the New Testament. Christ is the central figure of the Bible and the One the Hebrew Scriptures anticipate, hint at, and long for. As a result, these prayers are unapologetically *Christocentric*.

At the time of this writing, the Psalms are enjoying a historic revisitation in the broadest streams of the twenty-first-century Church. We hope the prayers offered in this book will contribute in some small way to a rediscovery of not only the Psalms, but the entire canon of Scripture.

Ultimately, our hope is that these prayers would lead you into the presence of the God who inspired the psalmists—the God who sanctifies the praise we bring and the ground on which we tread.

—*Ryan Whitaker Smith and Dan Wilt*

RIVER TREE

Lord,
Your presence is life to me:[1]
joy of my heart;
strength of my soul.

Grant me the grace to walk in Your ways;[2]
to cherish Your friendship
over the fellowship of the fallen,
soul-shaped as I am by the company I keep—
pressed and formed,
for good or for ill.

I refuse to march with those who mock Your mercy;
who revel in the unraveling of sacred things.
They stumble down trackless wastes,
training others in the ways of their wandering.

But You will be my delight, Lord;
Your Word my mirth and meal—
and I like an oak,[3]
drawing strength from fertile soil,
growing in grace,
safe in the circumference of Your mercy.

So I will flourish,
a river tree drinking from the deep—
fruit heavy on my branches;[4]
leaves thrumming with life.
Though seasons shift around me,
I will stand.

1. Ps. 16:11. 2. Ps. 86:11. 3. Isa. 61:3. 4. Gal. 5:22–23.

The godless are lifeless:
    withered stalks,
    bent by the wind;
such are those who shun Your mercy.
They forfeit seats at Your table,
refusing Your wedding garments;[5]
    choosing nakedness over grace.

I won't be counted among them—
not while Your River rushes for my good.

Lead me, Lord,
    strength upon strength,[6]
that at the end of my days I may look back
and wonder at the manifold mercy of God.

5. Matt. 22:1–14. 6. Ps. 84:5–7.

LORD OF NATIONS

Lord,
sometimes I am burdened by the politics of earth:
the serpentine plots of the proud;
the ruthless maneuvering of the underhanded
and double-dealing.

They writhe and seethe,
hungry for gain;
swarming like locusts at the harvest,
darkening the sun;
obscuring the Radiance of Your glory.[1]

But then I remember:
You are not threatened by their taunts,
and Your only proper response
is a high and holy laughter;
Your voice thunders from the heavens,
"Hear me, O great ones,
perched and playacting on your thrones:
there is but one King over all;
if you have eyes to see,
see Him lifted him up."[2]

Yes, Lord, I remember;
I call to mind the words of Your promise,
spoken in ages past to a godly king:
that from his offspring You would send Your Son
in the fullness of time[3]
to live and die among us,

---

1. Heb. 1:3. 2. John 3:14–15. 3. Gal. 4:4.

16

bearing the crucible of His cross,
and to rise,
bringing this world up with Him from the grave.[4]

Are not all nations and peoples Your rightful possession;
the ends of the earth Your just domain?[5]

Those who rule in wickedness
will be humbled before You;[6]
the power-hungry back-broken,
tossed into the street to beg for their dinner.

May all who reign and rule seek wisdom;
the proud be humbled;
the powerful bend their knees before Your throne.
May they know their own poverty,
that they might lay hold of the riches of Your grace.[7]

Indeed, the ground is level at the foot of Your cross,[8]
and all who kneel there,
peasant or king,
find rest for their souls.[9]

As for those who resist;
who cling to power with clenched fist—
they will be crushed beneath the heel.
Blotted out.
Expelled.
Forgotten.

For the rightful King returns for His throne,
and blessed are all who are washed in His blood.[10]

---

4. Rom. 6:4. 5. John 1:9–11. 6. Luke 14:11. 7. Eph. 1:7–10. 8. Gal. 3:26–29.
This phrase comes from the lyrics of a hymn. 9. Matt. 11:29. 10. 1 John 1:7.

HERALDS OF UNGRACE

Father,
why is it that the closer I get to You,
the more my enemies multiply?[1]
I am surrounded by a cloud of wicked witnesses—
scorners of wisdom;
heralds of ungrace.

But Your presence enfolds me,
shielding me from their poison tongues.
My eyes rise to meet Your gaze:
Delight of my Heart.[2]
Lover of my Soul.[3]

My words do not fall on deaf ears.
From broken whisper to deafening wail,
You hear me,
and from infinite realms of glory,
You stoop to reply.

As darkness descends,
I drift off to peaceful slumber,
safe in the arms of grace.
And when I wake,
I rise with new strength.[4]
The voices rattle on,
but their words have lost their hold on me.

Rise, Lord!
Lift me from their reach!

1. Ps. 38:19. 2. Song of Sol. 1:16. 3. Jer. 31:3. 4. Isa. 41:10.

Scatter their crooked chorus!
Shatter the jaws that utter lies!

You are the Way,
the Truth,
the Life,[5]
and all who love You are rightly called
the Beloved of God.[6]

5. John 14:6. 6. Song of Sol. 6:3.

ARCHITECT OF SALVATION

Lord God,
You are the Architect of My Salvation;
the one who began this good work in me.[1]
Do not be silent when I cry out to You;
when I lift my voice in the dark.
For Your words are comfort to me;
a steady hand on a restless heart.

Others mock me;
they don't understand;
they worship at the altars of their own eloquence,
filled with godless knowledge.

But You, Lord,
turn Your heart to the humble,[2]
drawing them unto Yourself.
You are not silent when we call,
desperate in our hour of need.[3]

The gods of the nations are deaf and dumb,[4]
but You see.
You hear.
You speak.

May I learn to practice wisdom—
restraining anger;
extending mercy.
By the working of Your Spirit
may I praise You as You rightly deserve—
entrusting my future to Your providence.

1. Phil. 1:6. 2. Prov. 3:34. 3. Phil. 4:19. 4. Ps. 135:15–17.

My present to Your mercy.
My end to Your grace.

I bristle at the discontentment of others:
those who are blessed,
yet beg for blessing;
who are clothed and fed by the hand of God,
yet refuse to bear Your cross,[5]
so at ease are they in their comforts.

But my roots run deeper;
You have filled me with the laughter of Heaven.
The wicked feast when fortune befalls them,
but I am at peace in Your presence.

You, Lord, are my joy—
not the blessings of Your hand;
the innumerable gifts of Your grace—
but You and You alone,
watching over me in the night,
like a mother with her child[6]—
whispering rest;
sheltering me with mercy.

5. Luke 14:27. 6. Ps. 131:2.

THE HOUSE OF GOD

God,
You are the One who sees and knows all things;[1]
who peers into the hearts of humankind
as if our souls were clear as glass;
who listens to the labored prayers
of saints and sinners alike.

In You are hidden all mysteries and knowledge;[2]
before You all creation is naked and bare.

Hear me, Lord;
hear my restless groaning.

I wake before the dawn,[3]
to carve a space for silence;
to meditate on Your words;[4]
to wait for the comfort of Your Spirit;[5]
the renewing of my strength.

You see the hidden shape of my heart:
my songs and sorrows;
victories and vices.

If I am proud,
make me humble.
If I am sinful,
make me chaste.
If I speak anything but the truth,
heal my words.

1. Job 28:20–24. 2. Col. 1:27. 3. Ps. 57:8. 4. Ps. 1:2. 5. 2 Cor. 1:3–4

By the miracle of mercy
I am ushered into Your house:
clothed in Your righteousness;
welcomed as a friend.[6]
You have filled me with joy and gladness;[7]
my tongue is loosed with praise.
You have loved me into life—
faithful in my wandering;
steadfast in my unrest.

Guide my steps, Lord;
lead me ever closer,
that those walking in death would see in me
such a witness of Your kindness
that they too might call upon Your name.

For their mouths condemn them;
they speak death as a first language,
cursing Your kingdom
and calling their hatred a love of religion.[8]

Christ, in Your great mercy,
Your arms are open to receive
all who freely come;
but those who reject You
shall find themselves rejected.
Those who spurn Your grace
will wander in a graceless land,
bent with sorrow,
while the children of God
feast in joy and song.[9]

---

6. John 15:15. 7. Ps. 100:2. 8. Inspired by a quote from G. K. Chesterton, essay in *Illustrated London News*, January 13, 1906, in *The Collected Works of G. K. Chesterton* (San Francisco: Ignatius Press, 1986), 27:100: "There are those who hate Christianity and call their hatred an all-embracing love for all religions." 9. Matt. 22:1–10.

You are the house about us, Lord—
a safe and secure place
in a world of crooked castles.
You have filled us with gladness,
welcoming us as daughters and sons;
seating us in places of honor,[9]
that we might be called the favored ones of God.[10]

9. Luke 14:10–11. 10. Ps. 90:17.

GOD OF THE LIVING

Father,
though You have cause to be angry
and are justified in Your displeasure,
do not turn Your face from me.[1]

Insofar as You are willing,
use my sin and the error of my ways[2]
as occasion for Your mercy;
my brokenness as grounds for Your healing.

For I am soul-sick and faint of heart,[3]
twisting and groaning in my bed.
I chant Your name in the dark,
but I am greeted with silence.

Come, Lord!
Save me from sleepless nights
and restless days;
from the reckless ruin of my own making.

Though I fall headlong,
I trust that You will catch me;[4]
that Your mercy is deep enough
even for me.

And when I have died a little,
I will rise again,
for You are God of the Living.
The dead pass on to the grave
and speak no more.

1. Ps. 102:2. 2. Ps. 51:3–6. 3. Ps. 27:14. 4. Ps. 91:9–12.

As for me, I will praise You,[5]
broken and weary as I am.

I lie in a pool of my own tears;[6]
are there any left to cry?
Am I dried up like an old wineskin—
thrown into a ditch,
shriveling in the sun?
My vision blurs,
my knees shake;
I am surrounded by enemies.

Be gone! All who oppress me—
you who have set your face against the Lord,
and torment the children of His promises.

For my Redeemer lives,[7]
and He comes swiftly to my rescue.
His silence is not indifference.
His discipline is not unkindness.[8]

He will stoop to lift me from the dust.
He will restore me,
while my enemies chase shadows in the dark,
blinded by the hand of God.

5. Ps. 42:5. 6. Rev. 21:4. 7. Job 19:25–27. 8. Prov. 3:11–12.

SHIELD AND SHADOW

Lord God,
I hide myself in You.[1]
Draw me from the dark;
steal me from this den of death,
before my soul is scraped hollow
and my hope is lost forever.

I'm charged with crimes I didn't commit;
burdened by the trespasses of others.[2]
They paint blood on my hands
and call me *"killer"*;
shove words in my mouth
and label me *"liar."*

If any of it is true,
let them have me.
If I'm guilty,
I'll take what I deserve.
Nothing is hidden from You[3]—
no secret uncovered;
no mystery concealed.

Show Yourself, Lord![4]
I'm pressed from all sides;
drawn downwards in despair.[5]
Bear Your sword;
drive this night away.

I look for Your arrival—
wreathed in fire,

1. Ps. 143:9. 2. Matt. 6:12. 3. Luke 8:17. 4. Ps. 18:25–26. 5. 2 Cor. 4:8–10.

the eyes of all turned upward in wonder
at the grandeur of Your glory.[6]

You weigh the world,
Measurer of Hearts;
start to finish,
beginning to end;[7]
history a breath
in the wind of eternity.

Uphold my cause, Lord;[8]
declare me innocent;
overthrow the violent.
Let me stand fast!

You are my Protector—
my Shield and Shadow;
Keeper of My Heart;[9]
Guardian of My Soul.

You bend Your bow
and Your enemies flee before You,[10]
falling into pits of their own making:[11]
diggers of their own graves.

I will not withhold my praise
or restrain my thanks.
Lifted by You,
I will lift Your name
and sing the glories of Your grace.

6. 1 Chron. 29:11. 7. Isa. 40:12. 8. Ps. 9:4. 9. Ps. 121:5–6. 10. Deut. 28:7.
11. Prov. 26:27.

FASHIONED FROM CHAOS

Creator God,
anoint my eyes with wonder
to behold the manifold witness of creation[1]—
Your name carved in every cell;
constellations brimming with glory;
the same Story told again and again,
in letters large and small.

At every turn, the miracle of life—
flesh shaped by the quickening breath of God:
a holy mystery,
met with silent awe
by even those who curse You.

I stand beneath the blanket of the skies,
heavy with a weight of glory,[2]
as moon,
stars,
supernovas,
distant galaxies,
sing in infinite night—
a deep space chorus
proclaiming Your goodness.

How is it, Lord,
that in Your power and majesty
You find time for me?
You—

1. Rom. 1:19–20. 2. 2 Cor. 4:17.

Spinner of Galaxies,
Sculptor of Space,
of Time,
of Matter,
make room to be Immanuel?[3]

In Your *"it is good"* world
You have called us *"very good"*[4]—
dust in the company of angels.

We are clothed in Your image;
christened as kings and queens
to rule with justice and mercy
over our small corner of creation—
to name.
Tame.
Create.
Grow culture from chaos.

You have placed us over all living things—
in land,
sky,
and sea[5]—
all bow before us
as we bow before You.

Hear, Lord!
hear the song of creation,
giving You praise.[6]

---

3. Matt. 1:23. 4. Gen. 1:31. 5. Gen. 1:26. 6. Ps. 148.

NATIVE TONGUE

Lord,
may gratitude be my native tongue,
and may I speak it well—
for all You have done
and all You have given—
word and object,
phrase and verse;
may I be fluent in the grammar of grace.

Enemies seen and unseen
scorn Your paths.
Stumbling,
they break their necks for lack of sense;
their memory a mist,[1]
lives lost in time.

You rule and reign over all:
King of Earth and Heaven,
avenging wrath and wrong;
forgiving and forgetting.[2]

You are a House for the homeless;
the Strengthener of the weak;
the Joy and Song of those who know Your name;
the Trust of every stalwart heart.

I will sing Your praise,
proclaiming the Story of Your Mercy
as long as I live:
that I am loved from eternity.

1. Ps. 73:20. 2. Mic. 7:19.

Bought with blood.
Raised to new life.[3]

When I am assaulted, Lord—
accused and attacked;
hemmed in by hatred—
draw me from the mire;
lift me to higher ground.[4]

The nations are a breath,
reigning in glory
until time makes fools of them all;
their cities, once lights of the world,
now buried in rock and clay,
while Your kingdom, Lord,
has no end.

You are the Hope of the desperate;
the Comfort of the afflicted;
the Joy of the redeemed.[5]

I praise You
for the working of Your will;
the kindness of Your grace.[6]

No one can stand against You:
awesome in power;
righteous in anger;
the One True King.

3. Col. 3:1. 4. Ps. 40:2. 5. Ps. 107:2. 6. Rom. 2:4.

UNTIL EVIL ENDS

Father,
if I may be so bold,
You have a habit of disappearing at the worst times,
when evil and cruelty are running rampant—
trampling the weak;
trafficking in flesh
and stolen innocence.
It is as if You withdraw;
turn Your face away.[1]

When will this madness end?
When will the captors be made captive,
imprisoned in the cells of their own devising?

See how they worship a lust
so base it should not be named;
how they covet gain,
fawning over it;
gluttonous in their greed.

So far removed are they from Your presence
that they don't spare You so much as a single thought.
They smuggle sin
and believe themselves to be free from its stain.

They flourish in godless ignorance,
swollen with easy profit;
pretending to be
immune,
immovable,
immortal.

1. Ps. 27:9.

Their tongues spew filth;
a steady stream of verbal excrement—
fluent in the language of blasphemy.

They build their crooked kingdom
on the backs of the oppressed.
Like ravenous animals,
they tear children from their mother's breasts.
They break the spirit of the innocent,
caging them like cattle;
selling their flesh for market value.

They spin sin like silk,
clothing themselves in the garments
of their own depravity.
They steal that which can never be restored;
break that which can never be healed—
and believe themselves to be free from guilt or shame.
For You have turned away
and pay them no mind.

When is enough enough, Lord?
How much misery can this world take
before You decide to act?[2]
Hear, Father—
hear the cries of the oppressed!
Their captors call You
Silent.
Aloof.
Dead.

But You see all things.
This blight upon the earth
will not have the last word.[3]
Is Your heart not with the humble and the weak?[4]

2. Ps. 13:1–2. 3. Prov. 19:21. 4. 1 Pet. 5:5–7.

Were You not made one with them in Your death—
splayed on a cross like a common criminal?
From the beginning,
You have taken the side of the oppressed.[5]
In You the orphan finds a father;[6]
the weary finds rest.

In time, You will execute judgment in the earth—
eradicating sin,
drawing its poison from every vein of creation
until all is made new.
You will reign,
King of New Beginnings,
and Your government will have no end.[7]

But how long, Lord?[8]
How long must we wait
until that slow kingdom comes?

See.
Hear.
Intercede for the broken in spirit.
Be Immanuel to all who suffer,
present in their pain.
Break their chains![9]
Lead them out with great rejoicing!

In Your mercy,
let this evil end at last.

5. Isa. 41:17. 6. Ps. 68:5–6. 7. Isa. 9:6–7. 8. Ps. 13:1–2. 9. Ps. 107:14.

THE PATH TO JOY

Father,
I long to be in Your house,[1]
in the shelter of Your presence;[2]
but with every step I take
I slip deeper into darkness.

I am chased in a godless land;
hunted like game—
every shot aimed square at my heart.
If evil triumphs
and the godly fall,
how can Your kingdom come?

Do You not reign in justice over all?
Is eternity not Your dwelling place?[3]
Do Your eyes not roam the world,
seeking those whose heart is Yours?[4]

With trials, You train the faithful—
pain a path to joy—
while the godless drink the wine of Your wrath
and suffer the silence of mercy.

Shunners of grace,
they will waste away,
while the children of God
shake free of these afflictions
and enter Your rest.[5]

1. John 14:2–3. 2. Ps. 91:1. 3. Isa. 66:1. 4. 2 Chron. 16:9. 5. Heb. 4:9–10.

THE STORY OF MERCY

How wide is Your mercy, Lord,
and how vast is its reach?
Can it storm the gates of hell?
Plumb the deepest dark?

Is there hope for the sons of Adam
and the daughters of Eve[1]—
or has the image of God been so defaced,
so marred beyond recognition,
that even Your mercy cannot heal it?

See how far we've wandered, Lord!
Our holy places are in ruins;[2]
our prophets in straitjackets.
We are double-minded,
double-hearted,
tossed like waves on the sea.[3]

We run our mouths,
railing against You;
hiding in haughty words.
Will You not tame these tongues
and mute us in Your mercy?

The broken and the vulnerable cry out day by day:
"Save us, O God!
The world is blind to us,
but You are the God of seeing."

1. "Sons of Adam" and "daughters of Eve" are phrases borrowed from
C. S. Lewis, *The Lion, the Witch and the Wardrobe* (1950; repr., New
York: HarperTrophy, 2000), 11. 2. Isa. 61:4–9. 3. James 1:6–8.

Yes, on account of them You will rise;
in the name of justice,
You will lift them from their labors
and show how great is the manifold mercy of God.

Your words are life to me:[4]
Spirit-breathed,
scribed by sinful saints
in ink and blood;
handed down,
generation to generation—
sacred wisdom;
the sprawling Story of Your Mercy.

You will not abandon us
in our despair.
You will rescue the humble in heart,
the poor in spirit.[5]
You will shelter us in a secret place.[6]
For wickedness runs rampant on the earth;
depravity a boundless blight.

But there is something deeper still,
a spell more fearsome than the curse:
how vast and wide is the love of Christ,[7]
and how unsearchable His riches.[8]

4. John 6:63.   5. Matt. 5:3.   6. Ps. 31:20.   7. Eph. 3:14–19.   8. Eph. 3:8.

A VOICE IN THE DARK

Lord,
I'm watching the clock,
as seconds
become minutes
become hours
become days,
and Your silence[1]
becomes a chasm I cannot cross.

Will it go on like this forever?
Will You clothe Yourself in shadow
and vanish on the wind?

I am left with my own thoughts;
weighed down with worry.[2]
Forsaken.
Forgotten.

Return to me, Lord;
lift this curtain of darkness.
Breathe life into my eyes
and light into my heart—
before the flame dims
and death snuffs it out.

I cling to Your goodness;[3]
it's all I have.
I lift my voice in the dark,
praising You for Your words,

1. Ps. 83:1. 2. Ps. 139:23–24. 3. Ps. 106:1.

though You are silent;
for Your nearness,[4]
though You are far.

For this affliction shall soon end,
and I will bear a weight of glory beyond compare.[5]

4. Ps. 145:18. 5. 2 Cor. 4:17–18.

THE SIDE OF THE REDEEMED

Lord,
I know You are there[1]—
though others doubt You,
foolish in their ignorance;
painting Your glory
with the brush of myth and legend.
They are lost in their confidence:
bent with sin;
unable to do good.

You survey the earth You've made,[2]
looking into the hearts of all;[3]
searching for those who understand;
who know what Story they are in—
those fumbling through the darkness
in the direction of the light.

No one is guiltless before You;
we've all been led astray[4]—
the best of us wandering from the path,
seduced by Sodom's song.

The enemies of Your Church
are ravenous in their hatred;
merciless in their arrogance;
summoning their own wisdom
as if it were the voice of God.

1. Ps. 139:7–12. 2. 2 Chron. 16:9. 3. 1 Sam. 16:7. 4. Isa. 53:6.

Their words will return to haunt them,
for You are on the side of the redeemed.

You, Lord,
are the Hope of the poor in spirit;[5]
the Refuge of the penitent heart.

I take comfort in the knowledge
that You will one day make all things new[6]—
rescuing the captives,[7]
healing the nations[8]—
and at the great wedding feast of the Lamb[9]
we will raise our glasses and rejoice.
Amen.

5. Matt. 5:3. 6. Rev. 21:5. 7. Luke 4:18–19. 8. Rev. 22:1–3. 9. Rev. 19:6–8.

A HILL OF THE HEART

There is a hill called *"Holy,"*
stark against a sky of fire;
a tabernacle of tree and stone,
where wind
and flame
and tremor
guard the gentle whisper of God.[1]

But who can tread that sacred ground?
Meet You in that hurricane eye?
Who can bear the closeness of the flame
at that celestial pole,
strung between earth and heaven?

The one who keeps to Your path
when others withdraw.
Who stockpiles truth in the hollows of the heart.
Who dispenses grace to friends and foes alike—
resisting evil,
cherishing good,
whatever the cost may be.

This, Lord, is my desire:
to be so rooted in Your ways
that I may not be shaken,
and by Your grace to meet You[2]
on Your holy hill.

1. 1 Kings 19:11–12. 2. Ps. 42:2.

GOD OF THE FEAST

Keep me whole, Lord,
for I've resolved to make my home with You[1]—
as You, though inhabiting eternity,
have stooped to make Your home with me.[2]

See how I've bet everything
on the word of Your promise:
that You are
Good.
Trustworthy.
True.

I thank You for the fellowship of the redeemed;[3]
the raucous symphony of saints;
this patchwork quilt of grace:
stitched,
frayed,
one.

Their faith gives me strength.
Together, we limp toward kingdom come.

This world is teeming with idols:
false messiahs promising temporary shalom
in dollar,
swagger,
flesh.
Their victims become shadows of their former selves—
emptied at the altar,
poured out like wax.

1. Ps. 90:1. 2. John 14:23. 3. 1 John 1:3.

Lord knows I've been there too,
more often than I'd like to admit—
but my heart,
weak as it is,
clings to You.

Are You not more than enough for me, Lord?
Do You not provide all that I need?
Your hand feeds me.
Your Spirit renews me.
Your blessing has made me rich,
and You add no sorrow to it.[4]

In Your mercy, You light my path.[5]
You speak to me in the stirring of my spirit.
In the flutter of my heart.
The chill of my spine.

Though I have run from You,
You remain;
ever present,
Faithful Friend.[6]
Trusted Guide.

I have no fear of the grave
or the sundering of my spirit from You,
for You have washed me in Your blood;[7]
clothed me in Your holiness;
and I will live to see the world made new.

You have shown me the way in which I must walk,[8]
and You choose to walk it with me.
The cheer of the damned is a thin draft
next to the rich ale of Your table;
the lusts of the flesh a scanty meal,
while the joy of the righteous is an endless feast.

4. Prov. 10:22. 5. Ps. 119:105. 6. Prov. 18:24. 7. Eph. 1:7–8. 8. Ps. 25:4–5.

JUSTICE PLEA

Hear me, Lord!
Hear my justice plea!
How it burns within me—
a fire in my bones;
a desperate cry in the dark.

Lying voices surround me,
within and without.
Though their time is short,
they chatter endlessly—
the frantic scheming of the damned.

Your presence is my only hope;
Your Spirit my sole comfort.
Tear the scales from my eyes.[1]
Be my vision.
Force all fear and foes to flee.
Deliver my soul from death.[2]

With careful steps,
I tread the path of life,[3]
eyes on You:
the Author and Perfecter of my faith.[4]

Guide me.
Direct me,
that I might not stumble into ruin.
Guard my tongue,
that it may speak truth.

1. Acts 9:18.   2. Ps. 116:8–9.   3. Ps. 16:11.   4. Heb. 12:1–2.

Guard my hands,
that they may do justice.
Guard my feet,
that they may keep to Your Path.

My spirit groans,
longing for Your nearness;
to be covered by the comfort of Your wings.
"Closer, Lord," I cry,
"draw closer still."

I refuse to settle for lesser loves—
passing comforts—
when You have promised to be present:
God With Me.
You held me in Your heart
before the world began.[5]

My deepest desire is to know You
in Spirit and in Truth;[6]
to be a friend of God.
To abide in You,
You in me,[7]
in intimate union;
closer than the bonds of blood.
To cling to You
as a child to its mother.[8]

I hear the celebration of the wicked—
the clinking of glasses;
the laughter of victory.
They revel in their power,
insatiable in their violence.

5. Rom. 8:29. 6. John 4:23. 7. John 15:5. 8. Ps. 131:2.

A lion lures its victim
by turns taunting,
then enticing,
until its teeth are in its flesh.
I listen as the beasts steal into my house,
circle my bed,
their mouths hungry for blood.

Scatter them, Lord;
with a shout, make them flee.
They will have their reward.

As for me,
I will seek Your face[9]—
the desire of my heart;
the end of all my sojourning.

9. Ps. 27:8.

THE DAWNING OF THE DAY

Lord Jesus,
You are my strength and my song.[1]
My heart swells at the thought of You—
My King.
My Ransomer.
My Righteousness.
The One in whom my life is hid,[2]
and in whom I,
though plagued with sin,
am born anew by Your blood.

I lift my voice in the dark;
You come swiftly to my rescue.

So entangled in death was I,
so coiled in sin;
banished from Eden;
severed from Your presence—
but You heard the cry of the fallen:
our stuttered prayers;
soul-sick yearning.
In the fullness of time[3]
You came among us
to raise the living from the dead.

Gentle and lowly in heart,[4]
a bruised reed You did not break;[5]
and yet the fire of justice burned within You.
You came in humility;

1. Ps. 118:14. 2. Col. 3:3. 3. Gal. 4:4–5. 4. Matt. 11:29. 5. Isa. 42:1–4.

in silent obscurity—
a birth hardly fit for a King.

But could we see beyond this terrestrial realm,
might we see You coming in glory,
the earth and all the heavens
quivering in fear and wonder,
the stars shrinking back—
as You,
in all Your splendor,
weave about You a thundering cloud of darkness,[6]
bending space and time as You descend;
planets trembling in Your gravity;
the infinite reaches of space expanding,
ever-expanding,
to make yet more room for the infinite love of God.

All dark and deathly things hide their faces;
all living things laid bare before You,
as the Maker of all things descends lower still,
and the Son of God,
Inhabiter of eternity,
steals into the dark of the womb.

The Word became flesh;
we beheld Your Glory.[7]
Through Your cross
and resurrection breath,
You have saved all who believe in Your name,
delivering us from the snare of death;
lifting us from the curse
we brought upon ourselves;
triumphing over the Enemy;
sheltering us beneath Your wings.[8]

6. Ps. 97:2. 7. John 1:14. 8. Ps. 91:1.

If not for Your grace,
I would have no place to stand.

You have rendered me righteous
on account of Your righteousness;
called me pure
in light of Your purity—
though I have not kept Your ways
and have fled from Your face,
scorning the statutes that lead to life.

Never have I been innocent;
shameless;
free from the burden of guilt—
but in Your mercy,
You fastened about me a garment of righteousness;[9]
a gift of glory
bought with blood.

Now, Lord,
grant me the grace to walk in Your ways:
to extend mercy,
cherish goodness,
strive for holiness,
and so draw closer to You.

For the poor in spirit will inherit Your kingdom,[10]
while the prideful are humbled in shame.

Your truth illumines all things,
scattering the dark;
bringing me to light.

You have filled me with new strength.
Breathed into me the air of Heaven.
Called me a New Creation.[11]

9. Isa. 61:10. 10. Matt. 5:3. 11. 2 Cor. 5:17.

Be praised, Lord!
For truth and beauty
and the endless glories of Your grace.
Truly You have covered me with Your kindness.

I am in awe of You
and all Your ways:
Strength illimitable.
Wisdom immeasurable.
Three Person'd God:[12]
alone in intimacy;
lavish in love.

You have breached the gulf of sin.
Broken Adam's spell.
Raised me from ruin.
Seated me in a place of honor.
Strengthened me for the fight.[13]

With might,
You have delivered me.
With kindness,
You have guided me.
With gentle whispers,
You build me up.
Through the power of Your Spirit,
I keep to Your paths.

The enemy desired to have me,
that he might sift me like wheat,[14]
but You have risen in victory over him—
crushing him beneath the heel;
lifting the curse that bound me.

12. Drawn from John Donne, "Holy Sonnet 14." 13. Eph. 6:12. 14. Luke 22:31.

Now I, in You,
have power to resist him,
along with all the saints;
and we will see the dawning of the day
when all the enemies of God
are gathered as fuel for the fire,
and the deceiver of all is cast into utter darkness,
while the children of God walk in Your favor;
the nations of the earth bow before You;
Your mercies made manifest.

All will choose their fate:
their will—or Yours—be done.[15]

I praise You, Lord,
for the Story of Your Mercy.
With blood, You have ransomed Your children
from every tribe, people, and nation.[16]
You have put a new song in our mouths.[17]
Filled us with the hope of New Creation.
Given us victory over sin.
Dominion over darkness.
Life over death.

You will reign forever,
and Your kingdom will have no end.[18]

15. Matt. 6:10. 16. Rev. 7:9–10. 17. Ps. 40:3. 18. Luke 1:32–33.

NIGHT AND DAY

The skies are charged with grandeur;[1]
Your glory carved in cloud and star:
a testament to Your goodness.

Day rouses from its slumber, announcing
Light.
Joy.
Hope.

Night follows in its wake, whispering
Rest.
Quiet.
Peace—
nature proclaiming
Your boundless power;
singular divinity:
a universal language.[2]

The dawn brings fresh mercies;[3]
a world made new.
At Your word,
light pierces the darkness;[4]
creation stirs.

The sun runs the arc of the world;
bounding over mountains,
spilling into valleys—
a warm blanket flung over the naked earth.

---

1. Inspired by the opening line of the Gerard Manley Hopkins poem
"God's Grandeur." 2. Rom. 1:20. 3. Lam. 3:22–23. 4. Gen. 1:3.

Your ways are righteous and true;
a fruit evergreen:
Reviving.
Renewing.
Transforming me,
from one degree of glory to another,
into the image of Christ.[5]

In You are the paths of life.[6]
Your words are sweet to my tongue;
my joy and delight.[7]
From seedtime to harvest,
in cold and in heat,
summer and winter,
day and night,[8]
I long to do Your will;
to walk in Your ways.
The grass withers,
the flower fades—
but Your word stands forever.[9]

My life is preserved by listening,
heeding,
following
Your commandments.
They are not far off;
they are near me—
In my mouth.
In my heart.[10]

You are holy.
Set apart.
Dwelling in unapproachable glory[11]—
and I am one of unclean lips.[12]

---

5. 2 Cor. 3:18. 6. Ps. 16:11. 7. Jer. 15:16. 8. Gen. 8:22. 9. Isa. 40:8.
10. Deut. 30:11, 14. 11. 1 Tim. 6:16. 12. Isa. 6:5.

The heart is deceitful above all things;
a tangled web of contradictions[13]—
but even there,
Your light shines:[14]
Cleansing.
Restoring.
Resurrecting.

May these words bless You, Lord;
may this heart-song magnify You:
Ground of all my hope.
Deliverer of my soul.

13. Jer. 17:9. 14. 2 Cor. 4:6.

THE BLESSING OF CHRIST

I bless you in the name of Christ
and ask that in His great mercy
He would not be silent when you cry out to Him—
that in the trials that await you
His presence would be near.
May you be surrounded by the ministry of Heaven
and the fellowship of the saints.[1]

Take comfort in this—
that the Father sees your heart;
how, despite many stumbles and falls along the way,
it stubbornly clings to His grace.

The dreams and desires within you are seen by Him:
your yearning for beauty;
your capacity for great and glorious things.
May He bring them to fruition!
May the garden you've been tending burst forth with life!
May you be a living example of the faithfulness of God
and the power of His Gospel.[2]

For He is not distant,
cloistered in a castle in the sky;
He is near—
Working.
Saving.
Redeeming.
Weaving a marvelous story with Your life.

1. Heb. 12:1. 2. Rom. 1:16.

While others hope in temporal things—
in power and privilege;
money and merit;
building houses on shifting sand[3]—
look once more to Jesus.[4]
Find in Him a deeper joy.

May your heart swell with the hope of New Creation,
anchored by the promises of God,
and so outlast these passing things.

Come, Lord Jesus,
bring us into Your eternal kingdom.
Amen.

3. Matt. 7:26–27. 4. Heb. 12:2.

PSALM 21

HEIR OF GOD

I am royal.
I am blessed—
a child of Almighty God.
An heir with Christ the King.[1]

You have raised me to new life[2]—
restoring desire;
aligning affections.
In losing myself,
I find myself in You.[3]

Sanctified by Your touch,
I hunger for holiness;
a Spirit-born bearing.[4]

You have crowned me with glory.[5]
Arrayed me in Your finest robes.
Given me a seat at Your table—
all because of Your relentless love;
Your persistent kindness to me.

Dying with You,
I rise with You—
united in Your resurrection;[6]
a child of eternity.
World without end.[7]

What love You have given me,
that I should be called a child of God.[8]

---

1. Rom. 8:17. 2. 2 Cor. 5:17; Rom. 6:4; 8:11. 3. Luke 9:24.
4. Rom. 8:14. 5. Ps. 8:5. 6. Rom. 6:5. 7. Derived from the *Gloria Patri*
(*Glory Be to the Father*) of liturgical tradition. 8. 1 John 3:1.

This mantle on my shoulders—
an honor fit for royalty—
is a gift I don't deserve.
I am a pauper in the house of the King.

You have delighted in me,[9]
surrounded me with Your faithfulness.
In Your presence, I find rest.[10]

May I trust You more and more,
loving You
with heart,
mind,
soul,
strength:[11]
a firm foundation beneath my feet.

You see through flesh and bone,
soul and spirit,
to sift between wheat and chaff,[12]
evil and righteous;
to reward all according to their ways.[13]

Your children will enter Your joy,[14]
while Your adversaries will be torn
from the book of the living;[15]
such is the fate of all who walk
as enemies of Your cross.[16]

You are kind.
Just.
Merciful.
Mighty.
Atoning Lamb.
Conquering King.

9. 2 Sam. 22:20. 10. Exod. 33:15. 11. Mark 12:30. 12. Luke 3:17.
13. Jer. 17:10. 14. Matt. 25:20–23. 15. Ps. 69:28. 16. Phil. 3:18.

How can I not worship at Your feet?
How can I not return Your kindness
with grateful praise?
For my sake
You were made to be sin
who knew no sin,
that in You,
I might become the righteousness of God.[17]
Amen!

17. 2 Cor. 5:21.

STRIPPED OF GLORY

Abba,
where have You gone?
In my greatest hour of need;
when all my strength has been wrung from me
like water from cloth,
You are nowhere to be found.
In turmoil, I cry out to You,
but my words return to me.

Once I was called the Beloved of God;[1]
a child of grace.[2]
Am I now orphaned by the One who sheltered me?
I am restless in Your absence.

My mind knows You are good
and worthy of all praise.
I recall the movements of Your mercy:
pillars of fire[3]
and covenant blood.[4]
The Word made flesh.[5]
Death undone.
The broken healed.
The needy rescued
by the gentle fury of Your love.

But look at me now:
Un-healed.
Un-answered.
Forsaken by God.

1. 1 John 3:1. 2. Eph. 1:4–6. 3. Exod. 13:21. 4. Exod. 24:8. 5. John 1:14.

I am the laughingstock of my neighbors;
a pitiful object of ridicule.
Perhaps it would be better to curse You
than to weep and plead
with no rescue.

Hear how the voices mock me:
"For all his faith,
he has seen no mountains moved,
no hills hurled into the sea.
If God is good,
then let Him save him—
or else put him out of his misery."

Are you not the One who made me?
Who breathed life into dust[6]
and spirited me into being?
Were You not nearer than the breasts that nursed me;
closer than my own flesh and blood?
Return to me, my Joy!
Lift me from my anguish!

I am a lamb among lions;
a calf thrown to wolves.
My enemies parade around me,
hungry for blood.

I am strung up;
gashed and gutted—
yet clinging to life;
palsied beneath the hunter's blade;
every nerve aflame.

The wicked close in,
lustful in their violence;
an angry horde of teeth and spittle.

6. Gen. 2:7.

They drive their stakes clean through me.
Strip me.
Mock me.

Abba,
if You can hear me,
let me know You're near.
You are my only hope;
my only chance of rescue.
Lift me from this den of hell.
Snap the cords that bind me.
Quickly, before it's too late!

What a story I would have to tell—
friends and family gathered round
to sing the glories of Your mercy.
Over bread and wine, we would proclaim
the relentless love of God,
which came among us in flesh and blood,
to triumph over death—
and triumphs still.

Give me the faith to believe
that You have not abandoned me in my pain.
In Your mercy, heal this blindness,
that I may live to see Your goodness yet again
in the land of the living.[7]

For You who suffered and died—
stripped of glory;
mocked for Your meekness—
are no stranger to pain.[8]
Were You not, in Your hour of need,
forsaken?[9]
Was Heaven not silent when You cried?
The sky speechless?

7. Ps. 27:13. 8. Isa. 53:3. 9. Mark 15:33–34.

Are You not now present with us
in our brokenness—
sharing our weakness?
Bearing our burdens?

Hear my prayer:
this stuttered hallelujah . . .
Feebly I proclaim,
this shall not be the end;
this crushing weight of sorrow will not endure forever.
For the old things will pass away[10]
and be remembered no more
when Abba comes to make all things new.

The tragic march of history will be over at last—
wars,
famines,
holocausts,
wasting disease,
inestimable loss,
forgotten,
when dawn breaks in Your new world.

On that day, there will be a feast,
as You gather Your children from the ends of the earth.
You will heal our brokenness at last;
all this pain and heartache
will be like a forgotten dream,
when You make Your home with us;
when Christ our King fills His cup;
and we all,
with one voice,
sing the Story of Your Mercy.

And our gladness will have no end.

10. 2 Cor. 5:17.

FURTHER UP AND FURTHER IN

Christ,
in Your presence I lack no good thing.[1]
You are the shepherd of my soul,[2]
guiding me to places of rest,
far from noise and clamor;
a meadow of the heart—
tall grass against an azure sky;
cooling waters at my side.
Lead me, Lord.
Further up.
Further in.[3]

When death looms like a specter over me
and I wander in a godless land,
speak comfort to me.
May Your Spirit be the light on my path;
the crook of Your staff guide me to safety.

With mercy, You lead me to Your table;
a feast of rich food and aged wine
in Your presence—
my Head and Host.
You delight in honoring me,
that all who see would know
I am the beloved of God.

1. Ps. 34:10. 2. 1 Pet. 2:25. 3. "Further up, further in" is a phrase borrowed from C. S. Lewis, *The Last Battle* (1956, 1984; repr., New York: HarperCollins, 2000), 205.

My head is blessed with oil;
my joy overflowing.

Your grace chases me.
Your kindness pursues me.
How can I outrun You?

In Your house are many rooms.
In Your presence I find rest.

A FOUNTAIN RUNNING OVER

Lord God,
all things are Yours—
all peoples and lands,
cultures and kingdoms,
granular sand and shimmering stars—
the walking,
talking,
swaying,
braying
dance of creation
is the happy work of Your hands
and Your rightful possession[1]—
breath-shaped from chaos;
spun into glorious order.

What does it take to be near You?
To lean upon Your breast,
close enough to whisper?

You have said, Lord,
that the righteous have an invitation to Your table;
that those washed in Your blood
are welcomed into Your house—
clothed in festive garments.
Seated at the feast.

By Your grace,
may I be counted among them—
for You give generously to all who ask,
and Your mercy is a fountain running over.

1. Deut. 7:6.

All who look for You find You,
and search no more.[2]

If every door knew its place,
it would open for You:
every holy,
solemn,
wretched,
royal space
unlatched,
unbarred—
from the flaming steel of Eden
to the vestibules of hell,
all would fling wide to give You passage.

For You are the rightful King
come back to claim His throne,
and You will not rest until
evil is vanquished.
Captives rescued.
Death undone.

Behold, the King of Glory comes!
And all knees will bend.

2. Jer. 29:13.

A HYPOCRITE HYMN

I am made for the heights of Heaven—
to soar above these passing things;
to look into the face of God[1]
and breathe the freshness of His grace.
Are You not the source of all my hope, Lord?
Is not my life built upon the Story of Your Mercy?

Lift me from the fray;
save me from the hands of God-mockers
and grace-scorners.
They will receive their just reward[2]—
while I wait patiently for You,
along with all who delight in Your appearing.[3]

See how my heart is open, Lord;
how I long to know the wisdom of Your ways;
the mysteries of Your mercy.

Have You not ransomed me with blood,
that I might draw closer,[4]
and closer still,
to the very heart of God?

In silence, I wait.

I feel the pull of my wayward feet,
earth-drawn as my soul strains heavenward.
How long will I sing this hypocrite hymn
and bear this double heart?

---

1. Num. 6:24–26. 2. Heb. 2:1–4. 3. 2 Tim. 4:8. 4. James 4:8.

But You, in Your mercy,
see above this house a stripe of blood,[5]
and forgetting all my fault,
judge me righteous:
a sinner with a saintly crown.

How great is Your kindness, Lord,
that You would rescue Your enemies
and call them friends!
The proud search, but do not find You,
while those who know their own poverty
find in You an endless feast,
journeying deeper and deeper
into the infinite love of God.

By Your grace,
You remember me at my best;
forget me at my worst;
and in gentleness, restore me.

Those who find You find life,
and wake in a world made new,
spending their days in wonder
at the miracle of mercy.

I have knelt before You,
naked in my shame,
and You have pulled me to my feet
and welcomed me home.
I fix my eyes on You,
confident in Your rescue.

When my soul is burdened
and all Heaven seems silent;

5. Exod. 12:12–13.

when the hope of New Creation
rings hollow in my heart—
Raise me up.
Restore me.
Give me a new song to sing.[6]

For I am attacked from all sides—
an object of loathing,
kicked about by the godless.

Protect me, Lord.
Rescue me from ruin.
Remember who You are to me:
Loving Father.
Faithful Friend.

Deliver me from this present darkness,
that I may sing the glories of Your grace.[7]

6. Ps. 96:1. 7. Eph. 1:6.

CLOAKED IN GRACE

Father God,
if I must be judged—
if every word and deed be weighed;[1]
all secret things unearthed and uncovered;
all shame laid bare—
I am confident that You will find me
innocent;
faultless;
without stain or blemish.

Perhaps I'll be called arrogant;
self-righteous;
a hypocrite.

The truth is, I have nothing to hide
that You have not redeemed.
To You, all hearts are open;
all desires known;
from You no secrets are hid.[2]

My debts have been paid,
down to the smallest white lie.
I am cloaked and covered in grace:
a righteousness not my own,
and so I stand righteous before You—
firm in Your love
and in Your faithfulness.

---

1. Prov. 21:2. 2. Episcopal Church, *The Book of Common Prayer and Administration of the Sacraments and Other Rites and Ceremonies of the Church* (New York: Oxford University Press, 1990), 355.

Help me to be mindful of the company I keep;
to sidestep those who cling to the dark;
to distance myself from poison tongues;
from those who delight in defiance of truth;
who worship empty things.

I return again and again to Your Story—
A spotless lamb slain.
A curtain torn.[3]
The tangled web of death undone.

I'm filled with gratitude—
cup overflowing;[4]
mouth loosed to sing Your praise.

What a joy it is to see Your people gathered;
to join in the song of the redeemed.[5]

I know my own weakness, Lord.
Keep an eye on these wandering feet;
don't let me fall back into darkness,
subsumed in crooked company—
sliding down with the godless and the insolent
into the pit of their own making.

No, Lord;
that is not my destiny,
nor my destination.
I am determined to keep to Your path;
to stay the course;
to remain in Your love.
Son of God, have mercy on me, a sinner.[6]

I stand on Your promises;
lean on Your grace;
and with all the saints

---

3. Matt. 27:51. 4. Ps. 23:5. 5. Rev. 5:9–10. 6. Derived from the Jesus
Prayer of liturgical tradition.

I sing the breadth
and length
and height
and depth
of the love of God.[7]

7. Rom. 8:38–39.

LIGHT AND LIFE

Lord Jesus,
You are Light and Life.[1]
Illuminator of inner and outer worlds.
Beacon in starless night.
Lamp on twisting path.[2]
Breath of life in every living soul.[3]

You have delivered me from sin and death;
raised me to new life with You.[4]
There is no darkness so deep,
no evil so strong,
that it can wrest me from Your presence.[5]

Still,
forces gather on the horizon[6]—
rank upon rank,
ravenous in their hatred,
waging war while I walk these shadowlands.
Avert their eyes, Lord;
confuse their plans;
let no weapon formed against me prosper.[7]
May safety surround me—
Sabbath rest in the storm.

In the end,
there is only one thing of lasting worth;
one desire that burns within me:
that I would continually live
in,
through,
from,

1. John 8:12.   2. Ps. 119:105.   3. John 1:4.   4. Rom. 6:4.   5. Rom. 8:38–39;
Ps. 139:11–12.   6. Eph. 6:12.   7. Isa. 54:17.

the center of Your love,
dwelling in the secret place;
perceiving Your wonder;
beholding Your beauty;
meditating on Your goodness.

In trouble,
You usher me into
a room prepared for me—
fire in the hearth,
feast on the table,
a home of the heart.[8]

In Your presence,
my soul is refreshed;
my hanging head lifted;
my trembling heart quieted,
as songs rise up in me again:
grateful praise for saving grace.

Help me to know that You are near, Lord;[9]
that my cries don't fall on deaf ears;
that these prayers aren't lost on the wind.

Quiet my heart to hear Your voice.
Give me clear direction;
confident trust.

Am I not led by Your Spirit?
Am I not a child of God?[10]
I cling to the promise that You see and know
before I even ask.[11]

I lift my eyes to the sky—
stars shimmering in the blanket of night.

8. John 14:23; Rev. 3:20. 9. Ps. 30:10. 10. Rom. 8:14. 11. Matt. 6:8.

I am Orion,
hunter in the dusk,
seeking truth in a world of shadow.

At every turn,
I find You:
Living Word.[12]
Radiance of Glory.[13]
Light of the World.[14]

But I see in passing glance
and dim reflection.
How I long to behold You in Your glory—
not through a glass darkly,[15]
but as a friend sees a friend:
face to face.[16]

Do You hide Yourself?
Do You reject me because I run from You?
Perhaps it is I who am hiding,
and You who are running after me.[17]

Never have I been forsaken;
never have You left me.
Silently,
steadily,
You have worked Your will in me.
When those closest to me had no power to help,
You remained faithful;
Your hand provided.

I waver between faith and doubt,
fearful of Your turning away—
that I will be cast off;
disinherited from Your promises.

12. John 17:17. 13. Heb. 1:3. 14. John 8:12. 15. 1 Cor. 13:12. 16. Exod. 33:11.
17. Henri Nouwen, *Return of the Prodigal Son: A Story of Homecoming* (New York: Continuum, 1995), 106–7.

I return to the firm foundation of Your truth:
that Your Spirit dwells within me,
the hope of glory;[18]
that You are with me,
to the end of the age;[19]
that Your presence is proved
by steadfast love
and endless mercies.[20]
My fear,
doubt,
worry,
cannot alter this reality.

Shield me from darkening dangers;
from lying voices—
enemies known and unknown.
Protect me from the curses of their mouths.
Give me a response in my hour of need.[21]

I hold to the promise of Your faithfulness—
that I will see some good before the end:
that it is my portion;
my cup overflowing.[22]

You are not slow to fulfill Your promise,
but are patient in Your mercy,[23]
preparing a weight of glory beyond compare.[24]

Quiet my heart;
grant me patience in these afflictions.
May faith arise in me
as I draw near to You
and wait to see You move.
Amen.

18. Col. 1:27. 19. Matt. 28:20. 20. Lam. 3:22–23. 21. Ps. 119:42; Luke 12:12.
22. Ps. 23:5. 23. 2 Pet. 3:9. 24. 2 Cor. 4:17.

WIND AND WORD

Oh Christ,
help me to know You are near.
I can suffer pain,
rejection,
the loss of many precious things—
but if You are silent;
if Your voice is lost to me,
I don't know if I can bear it.

For as long as I can remember,
You have spoken to me—
in whisper,
ache,
and tear;
in wind and word:
a language of the heart.
Without that tethering thread
I would be utterly lost—
a cave-dweller,
a stranger to the light.

These days it feels like I'm sending messages into the void—
a scrap of parchment in a bottle;
a lone lantern sailing into the dark—
as if I could reach You;
as if I could somehow steal into the place Your glory dwells.[1]

Have mercy, Lord.
Comfort me.
Speak.

1. Ps. 26:8.

I am not like those who have no hope.[2]
I won't be counted among the Lost Ones—
who toil and spin for prideful gain;
who bless with the mouth and curse with the heart.[3]

Mocking Your mercy,
they will be judged by their own works;
for we have all fallen short of Your glory,[4]
and they will be measured by the distance of the fall.

You have been silent to me for a time,
but they say You have never spoken.
They have turned their faces from You,
content with empty knowledge.
They will be like a house torn down to the studs;
scraps sold for a bargain price.

As for me, I am comforted.
In the darkness, a glimmer of light appears,
as the Morning Star draws the dawn:[5]
Christ, my only hope.
My sole defense.
My confidence and courage.

I languish—
You lift.
I reach—
You rescue.
Such is the song of the redeemed.

You are faithful to Your children, Lord,
holding us with a strength greater than our own;
ransoming us from every tribe and tongue;[6]
leading with love;

2. Eph. 2:12–13. 3. James 3:10. 4. Rom. 3:23. 5. Rev. 22:16. 6. Rev. 5:9.

that we might carry Your kindness,
generation to generation,
as You carry us, Lord.
Amen.

LIVING WORD

Living Word,[1]
enthroned upon grateful praise,[2]
glorified by hosts of Heaven,
seen and unseen—
creation testifies to Your glory:
all made through You and for You,[3]
who are before all things,
and in whom all things hold together.[4]
I marvel to think that I,
one with unclean lips,
have seen the King.[5]

Bless the Father, O my soul—
thundering voice of creation;
Artist of order,
reality upheld by the word of Your power. [6]

Bless the Son, O my soul—
Heaven's ascended Lord.
A bruised reed You did not break,
but with a loud voice You cried,
"It is finished,"[7]
and the foundations of the earth were shaken;
creation trembled before its King.[8]

Bless the Spirit, O my soul—
Wind of God's glory among us;
Tongue of Fire in our midst;[9]
Tamer of desolate lands
and wayward hearts.

1. John 1:1–4. 2. Ps. 22:3. 3. Col. 1:16. 4. Col. 1:17. 5. Isa. 6:5. 6. Heb. 1:3.
7. John 19:30. 8. Matt. 27:51. 9. Acts 2:3.

You speak life into the darkness of the womb;
the cruel Winter gives way to Spring.
You lay waste mountains.[10]
Open rivers on bare heights.[11]
Your people bow in wonder,
with all the saints,
proclaiming,
"Holy, Holy, Holy,
is the Lord God Almighty,
who was
and is
and is to come!"[12]

You reign over all:
Regent of Creation.
Guarder of Holy Mysteries.
Sustainer of Cellular Song.

Father.
Son.
Spirit:
Living Word—
Above me.
Below me.
Around me.
Within me.[13]
Strengthen my heart today;
lead me in the path of peace.[14]
Amen.

---

10. Isa. 42:15. 11. Isa. 41:18. 12. Rev. 4:8. 13. Col. 1:27; this line reso-
nates with "St. Patrick's Breastplate" (*Lorica*) of the Irish prayer tradition. 14. Prov. 3:17.

DRAWN FROM DEATH'S DOOR

Lord God,
as much as this feeble heart can manage,
may it exalt You today.

I am numbered with the redeemed;
an heir of endless grace—
lifted from the well;
drawn from death's door.

The enemy longed to have me,
but You heard the cry of my heart.
In Your mercy, You wrestled me from his hands—
restored me;
renewed me;
annulled death's claim on me.
You have raised me up—
a New Creation,
one with Christ.

I'm overwhelmed with gratitude.
How can I not sing this song as long as I live?
I cannot escape Your mercy.
Once I felt Your face turned away from me,
but now I see You.
Once we were enemies.
Now I sit at Your table.

Sorrow can feel like endless night,
until the sun rises with healing in its wings,[1]
to tell Your Story again.

1. Mal. 4:2.

And yet—
sometimes I forget.

When things are well with me;
when I'm content and comfortable,
rich with the blessings of Your hand,
I can lose my way—
step by step,
a gentle wandering—
until I've lost the path,
and darkness surrounds me.

Once again, I fall on Your grace—
voice a fragile prayer;
a flicker in the infinite night.

Surely You haven't saved me to leave me here;
ransomed me with blood
to cast me aside.
If death has the final word,
what good is Your salvation?
Hear me:
Kyrie eléison.
Christe eléison.[2]

You are faithful always—
my Good Shepherd.[3]
How often have You lifted me from the brambles;
cradled me in the comfort of Your arms;
carried me to safety?
You throw a party for Your lost and found one—
a homecoming celebration.[4]

---

2. A transliteration of the Greek version of the liturgical prayer,
"Lord, have mercy; Christ have mercy." 3. John 10:11, 14–15. 4. Luke
15:3–7, 21–24.

In Your joy,
I forget my sorrow.
In the light of Your face,
I remember Your mercy.
With songs of deliverance,[5]
You unwind my wandering;
forget my faithlessness.

God forbid I should keep quiet.
I will praise You as long as I live.[6]
In weakness, I will exalt You,
until I am raised imperishable.[7]
Amen.

5. Ps. 32:7. 6. Ps. 63:4. 7. 1 Cor. 15:52.

COVENANT KEEPER

Father,
my life is a story
of Your relentless faithfulness to me[1]—
a story of how we have walked
through this world—
You, the Covenant Keeper;[2]
I, the Covenant Kept.

Once again,
I come to You in need,
desperate for deliverance.
Where else can I go,
when You have the words of life?[3]

If I live,
may I live for Your glory.
If I die,
receive my spirit
as I have received Yours:
a willing sacrifice;
a cruciform love.

Worship shatters the idols
that contend for Your throne:
hungry gods demanding allegiance.
They are parched,
but never quenched;
lustful,
but never satisfied.

1. Lam. 3:22–23. 2. Deut. 7:9. 3. John 6:68.

With empty promises,
they lead me deeper into myself,
until I am alone with my desires;
a terrifying proposition.

Twisted in their lies,
Your Name becomes lost to me:
a distant memory;
a word out of reach.
They preach a religion of forgetfulness,
by turns stealing,
killing,
destroying.[4]

And so I wear grief like a garment;
sadness like a heavy robe.
Where once Your goodness and mercy followed me,[5]
now I am chased by fear and worry:
a brooding cloud—
expanding,
deepening,
as friends withdraw,
and vision fades,
and I am lost in the mist,
left to chattering voices
and my own self-loathing.

May I remember Your mercy, Lord,
and rejoice once more in You.
In this endless night,
Your grace is a wide-open space;[6]
a sunlit glade
beneath a cloudless sky;
a place to run,
unhindered;

4. John 10:10. 5. Ps. 23:6. 6. Ps. 18:19.

to dance,
uninhibited.

But I am sick with grief.
I fear the darkness will overtake me;
that in the witching hour,
I will vanish from the earth—
my soul so splintered and spent;
my body so wracked with pain
that I will pass from the land of the living
into hopeless oblivion.

You have said my name is
hidden in Your heart;
etched on a white stone.[7]
But here, I am known as
"Forgotten."
"Rejected."
"Humiliated."
What a cruel twist of fate,
when all I wanted
was for others to see You in me.

Still,
I believe You are good.
I have held to that truth
relentlessly,
stubbornly,
in spite of my own fear and doubt;
in defiance of those who have cursed me—
who have called You a liar;
me a fool for trusting You.

Have You not promised to draw near to me
when I draw near to You?[8]

7. Rev. 2:17. 8. James 4:8.

To cover me in the shadow of Your wings;[9]
in the shelter of Your keeping?
To shield me from the vengeful;
from those whose portion is in this life?

Lead me to the secret place,[10]
beyond the reach of their voices,
lest their lies become a shroud about me;
a shameful covering.

If not for Your faithfulness, Lord,
I would be lost.
You have kept Your end
of this blood bond.
You are the Provider of the sacrifice.
The flaming torch of covenant.
A ram in a thicket.[11]
A lamb led to slaughter.[12]

In my anguish,
You hear me.
You send Your angels to comfort me:
a Heavenly battle guard.
Your favor has won my heart.

Covenant Keeper,
in this restless world,
may I stand fast:
a testimony to Your faithfulness;
a Covenant Kept
in an age of broken promises.

9. Ps. 57:1. 10. Ps. 91:1. 11. Gen. 22:13–14. 12. Isa. 53:7.

THE FACE OF MERCY

Father,
it is a good thing to be loved by You;
to receive Your free gift;
to put on Christ.
The record of my sins has been nailed to the cross;[1]
utterly forgotten;
cast behind Your back,[2]
flung the distance of East to West.[3]

But I am forgetful.
I have stumbled and staggered,
drawn to sin like moth to flame—
hands cupped round the flickering wick,
that You might not put it out.

I have played with fire,
too enraptured to feel the burn.
Such is sin held in:
it ravages within.

Like one bent with grief,
I twisted and turned,
while grace rapped on the door,[4]
demanding entry.
Such was my resistance,
until, unable to bear it,
I opened my heart,
laying it before You:
the full weight of my wandering.

1. Col. 2:14. 2. Isa. 38:17. 3. Ps. 103:12. 4. Rev. 3:20.

You took my hand,
Your touch a more ravishing flame
than that which ruined me,
and said,
"All that is forgotten now."

If only everyone called by Your name
would behold the face of mercy;
know the depths of grace;
carve a space for silence,
patient for Your presence—
in poverty of spirit
and hopeful expectation.

How quickly I forget
how safe I am with You, Lord—
held by Your hand;
comforted by Your kindness.
Defended.
Delivered.

Your voice speaks life to me,[5]
calling me to higher things.
Long-suffering Lord,
though I am slow to learn,
teach me.
Though I am quick to sin,
rebuke me—
until I walk with steadier step
and undivided will.

Trouble follows the disobedient;
the ground of the godless is cursed—
thorns and thistles
choking heart and soul.

5. John 6:63.

As for me,
I find mercy at every turn;
hope in the darkest of places.
Your kindness encircles me.
Your joy uplifts me.

May all Your people praise You;
all those brought from death to life,
with one voice
sing the song of Your salvation.[6]

6. Ps. 118:15–16.

THE SOUND OF JOY

Joy! For the beauty of Your holiness![1]
Joy! For the constancy of Your truth![2]
Joy! For the might of Your justice![3]
Joy! For the goodness of Your heart![4]

With all the citizens of Heaven
I sing the wonders of Your name—
with key,
string,
drum,
voice—
a merry racket;
grateful praise for all You have done.

Creation testifies to Your faithfulness,
groaning to be filled with Your knowledge[5]
as the waters cover the sea.[6]
In that day,
the nations will know Your glory;[7]
all wars will end;
all tears will dry;[8]
death will be a distant memory;
as the sound of joy draws us—
host upon host of angel choirs
singing *"Holy"*;[9]
Your children shining like the brightness of the sky;
like stars in the heavens,[10]
with nothing left to steal our joy.[11]

---

1. Ps. 29:2. 2. John 8:32. 3. Ps. 89:14. 4. Titus 3:4–7. 5. Rom. 8:22. 6. Isa. 11:9.
7. Isa. 62:2. 8. Rev. 21:4. 9. Rev. 4:8. 10. Dan. 12:3. 11. John 16:22.

Joy!
For in the beginning,
You quieted the waters of chaos;
breathed life and light into creation:
Your handiwork—
laced with holy mystery,
as unfathomable as the depths of the seas;
as rains hidden in the heavens.
Waters gather upon waters—
snow and rain,
hail and sleet,
cloud
and mist
and fog;
truly we see through a glass darkly.[12]

Joy!
For I walk by faith,
not by sight.[13]
Grant me the gift of awestruck wonder,
that I may learn the limit of my knowledge;
the number of my days;[14]
and trust You,
leaning not on my own understanding.[15]

With great effort, I turn a phrase,
but Your words make worlds.

Joy! For the beauty of Your holiness!
Joy! For the constancy of Your truth!
Joy! For the might of Your justice!
Joy! For the goodness of Your heart!

Joy!
For Your promises outlast empires.

12. 1 Cor. 13:12. 13. 2 Cor. 5:7. 14. Ps. 90:12. 15. Prov. 3:5.

The rulers of the earth plot and scheme,
forgetting that their lives are but a vapor,
a passing mist;
while Your word abides,
unchanging;
Your purposes,
unthwarted.
May no one miss their moment
to find You;
praise You;
walk with You.
Blessed are all who are called to be
citizens of Heaven.

You are the God of Seeing.[16]
No creature is hidden from Your sight;
all are naked and exposed before You.[17]
Every life precious in Your eyes—
a painting in progress;
a song to be sung.
In Your mercy,
You lead us to wells of salvation,[18]
to springs of Living Water[19]—
Your body and blood
our true food and drink.[20]

Your joy is an ambling brook;
a river of gladness streaming from Your throne.[21]
My soul finds rest in its waters.
I delight in trusting You.

Joy! For the beauty of Your holiness!
Joy! For the constancy of Your truth!
Joy! For the might of Your justice!
Joy! For the goodness of Your heart!

16. Gen. 16:13. 17. Heb. 4:13. 18. Isa. 12:3. 19. John 4:10; 7:38; Rev. 7:17.
20. John 6:55. 21. Ps. 46:4.

ILLUMINED BY LIFE

Father,
may every word on my tongue
be one of thanks to You;[1]
every thought in my mind
a meditation on Your goodness.
All I am,
all I have,
is from Your hand—
You, the Giver;
me, the happy recipient of breath and bread;
of beauty, joy, and grace.

The wise among us know their own poverty;
their unpayable debt to You.
The only response is gratitude:
heartfelt thanks for all You have done.

But You are not only Provider;[2]
not only Lord;
You have condescended to dwell with us[3]—
a knowable God.
I have reached for You
and found You.
I have known the comfort of Your Spirit;[4]
the tenderness of Your mercy.
I have traded my worries
for the peace of Your presence.

I am illumined by Your life,
Your face shining upon me:

1. Ps. 30:12. 2. Gen. 22:14. 3. John 1:14. 4. John 14:26–27.

a dim mirror,
awaiting glory.
How could I turn back to what I once was?

I was just a beggar at the door of grace,
but You welcomed me in;
heard my story;
offered me a seat at Your table;
commanded the hosts of Heaven
to watch over me.[5]
I am a permanent guest in the house of God—
a beneficiary of infinite kindness.
In Your presence I lack nothing.[6]

If only all could trust in Your goodness—
would they not be ushered in as I have been?
Awed by Your glory,
quieted by Your presence?
So many starve outside the banquet hall,
while the doors are open,
and the table is set.

The secret of the universe
is not so difficult to find.
I could tell it in simple verse;
in a song;
in a children's tale.
You have set life and death before us:[7]
the sweet and bitter fruit—
our choice.

Everywhere I look,
I see people searching for life
in all the wrong places;
planting seeds in shallow soil.[8]

5. Ps. 91:11–12. 6. Ps. 23:1. 7. Deut. 30:19–20. 8. Matt. 13:5–6.

Do they not all long for You,
unconscious desire burning within them?

As for me,
I have resolved to walk in Your ways;[9]
to tell the truth
with mouth,
hands,
feet:
a living witness to Your mercy.

You are everywhere,
but nowhere so much as with Your children:
Faithful Father.
Righteous Redeemer.
By Your light, we see.

But those who have shunned You—
who cling to darkness
while infinite joy is offered them—
will suffer the harshness of the dark lands,
shadowed by Your turning away.

You are the night watchman of
Your blood-bought children;
the shepherd of Your flock.[10]
Savior of the afflicted,
the scorned,
the forgotten.

We are burdened,
but not crushed;
struck down,
but not destroyed.[11]

9. Ps. 25:4. 10. Isa. 40:11. 11. 2 Cor. 4:8–9.

These momentary sufferings
prepare us for glory.[12]

One with Christ,
we are patient in our afflictions,[13]
awaiting the day when the last enemy falls,
sorrow flees away,
and we look with fresh eyes on a world made new.

All who walk in death
worship death,
become death,
suffer death.

In the end,
only the ransomed will remain:
children at the feast of God—
the humble exalted;
the proud humbled;
the King of New Creation glorified.
Amen and Amen.

12. 2 Cor. 4:17–18. 13. Rom. 12:12.

STRONG LORD

You are the Strong Lord.
I stand my ground
on the battle line—
firm in Your love;
grace;
volition.

In the power of Your Spirit[1]
I face down enemies
within and without.
You don't mince words
with the wicked:
those who harass the humble;
who ridicule the righteous.

You are the Guardian of the Graced;
the Champion of the Chosen;
the One who goes before us;[2]
who fights on our behalf.

A storm breaks on the horizon:
heavy clouds darkening the sun;
wind and rain dragging hell behind them.

Come, Breath of God!
Raise a thunder army—
a wind chorus of horse and chariot[3]
to drive this darkness away.
May hosts of Heaven
war against them on my behalf,

1. Zech. 4:6. 2. Deut. 31:8. 3. 2 Kings 7:6.

bearing me up
in the midst of the fray.

I am hopeless without You.

I praise You, Lord,
for You have delivered me from death's door;
raised me from ruin.
You are the Deliverer of the Poor.
Father of the Fatherless.[4]
Strengthener of the Weak.[5]
There is none like You.[6]

I have tried to extend Your kindness to others—
weeping with those who weep;[7]
walking with the broken;
interceding for the oppressed—
only to be met with betrayal.
In remaining faithful to You,
I am called faithless.
In keeping to Your path,
I am called aimless.

I have prayed in the secret place
that Your goodness and mercy
would follow those who have cursed me.
I have extended mercy,
while they have doled out judgment.

Gratitude keeps me grounded;
restores my confidence
in the good work You have begun in me.[8]
You will never leave me or forsake me.[9]
Your discipline,
though painful,
yields the peaceful fruit of righteousness.[10]

4. Job 29:12. 5. Ezek. 34:16. 6. 1 Sam. 2:2. 7. Rom. 12:15. 8. Phil. 1:6.
9. Heb. 13:5. 10. Heb. 12:11.

How does one speak truth in trying times?
When all follow their own way,
gathering to themselves mentors
to suit their own passions?[11]
How does one build where others have torn down?
Speak Life where Death is the native tongue?
When I speak in blessing,
the world turns its back on me,
claiming,
with rank contempt,
that they have moved on from childish things.

I am not concerned with my own defense—
they can take me or leave me—
only let them see You, Lord,
in all Your glory.
The Word Made Flesh,
who tabernacled among us:[12]
our only hope.
Be lifted high;
be praised as You deserve.

If it brings You honor,
defend me.
If it brings You fame,
intercede for me—
only let them see Jesus in me.
May they be ashamed of their careless words.
May they repent of their lawlessness.

Not all is lost.
There are some who remain faithful;
who help me bear this heavy load;
who run with endurance—

11. 2 Tim. 4:3. 12. John 1:14.

eyes locked on You,[13]
eager for the crown of life.[14]

I am a sojourner here;
an exile in a foreign land.
But I will praise You all the more,
for each day,
each hour,
each breath You give.

13. Heb. 12:1–2. 14. Rev. 2:10.

PATIENT CHRYSALIS

Lord God,
protect me today from the lies of the enemy.
I have seen too many friends stumble into darkness,[1]
following the winsome voice of death;
defacing Your image
piece by piece,
until You lay no further claim upon them.

They become what they worship,[2]
feeding their lust in secret:
a shrine to a hungry god.
With twisted rhetoric they suppress the truth,[3]
forgetting that You see and know all things;
that nothing escapes Your notice.

Yes, Lord—
many friends have fallen away.
They have traded Your wisdom for the wisdom of the world—
calling good evil
and evil, good;[4]
darkness, light;
bitter, sweet.

If I could measure Your goodness,
would it not fill creation?[5]
Everywhere I look I see the mercies of God—
in mountain peak,
pillared cloud,
swirling waters;
all created things
singing Hallelujah.

1. Prov. 4:18–19. 2. Ps. 135:15–18. 3. Rom. 1:18. 4. Isa. 5:20. 5. Eph. 4:10.

I am in awe of Your goodness.
You save to the uttermost
all who come to You.[6]
You cover them in Your kindness—
rags to righteousness—
shielding them from the sting of death.
You seat us in places of honor
at Your never-ending feast;
we go from glory to glory.[7]

Even as our bodies waste away,
we are being renewed[8]—
a patient chrysalis
waiting for New Creation—
to walk with You in the cool of the day,
with no need of sun or moon.[9]

Watch over me this day, Father;
keep me in the path of life.[10]
May love and mercy guide me;
the fellowship of Christ center me.
I am bent toward pride,
weak of will.
May Your Spirit guide me
away from wrack and ruin—
the easy paths of the dead.
Step by step they descend
in the gathering dusk,
until darkness envelops them
and they are no more.

6. Heb. 7:25. 7. 2 Cor. 3:18. 8. 2 Cor. 4:16. 9. Rev. 21:23. 10. Ps. 16:11.

YOU ARE WISDOM

Lord,
You are Wisdom.
I sit at Your feet.
I choose the Way of Grace.

Envy raps at my door[1]—
evil flourishes;
goodness is in short supply.
I hold my ground,
recalling the riches of Your promises,
for darkness will not have the final word.

Trust is a song in my soul—
may I walk faithfully with You,
doing justice;
loving kindness;[2]
colonizing Earth with the presence of Heaven.[3]

Delight is a spring of living water—
for You are the hope of my heart;
the end of all my longing.

Commitment is the path before me—
a slow sanctification;
glory to glory;[4]
a patient harvest of righteousness.[5]

Stillness is my practice—
silence, my companion.

---

1. Gen. 4:6–7. 2. Mic. 6:8. 3. Inspired by a phrase from N. T. Wright, *Surprised by Hope* (New York: HarperOne, 2008), 293. 4. 2 Cor. 3:18. 5. 2 Cor. 9:10; James 3:18.

May fear and worry find no resting place in me;
let me not long for the busy blessings of the wicked.

Restraint is my shield—
a guard around my heart.
May I not be driven by desire;
ruled by resentment.
Such is the way of the world
that passes away
along with its longings,
while those who do Your will
abide forever.[6]

Meekness is my choice[7]—
peace, my quiet reward.

Laughter is healing to my bones—
I join in Heaven's joy;
a righteous revelry—
for the kingdoms of earth
and the powers of hell
will not endure forever.
All death and darkness,
cruelty and captivity,
are but a slight digression;
a passing mention
in the Story of Mercy.

Contentment is a stabilizing grace—
the godless are gluttons for gain,
collapsing under the weight of their want,
while You exalt the humble.[8]
In You I lack no good thing.[9]

Righteousness is fanned into flame within me—
like the light of dawn,

6. 1 John 2:17. 7. Matt. 5:5. 8. Matt. 23:12. 9. Ps. 34:10.

it shines brighter and brighter until full day.[10]
I wait for New Heavens and a New Earth
where righteousness dwells.[11]

Poverty heightens my awareness
of the depths of my need.
I am awakened to my weakness;
aware of Your strength.
I walk in the power of Your Spirit,
fed with bread from Heaven.[12]
You fill the hungry with good things,
while the full are sent away empty;[13]
the godless are a passing mist.

Inheritance is my birthright—
I am a child in the house of God:
accepted,
embraced,
while the wicked weep and gnash their teeth.[14]

Faithfulness is a guard about me—
as I walk with You,
stumbling and staggering,
You make straight my paths;[15]
You stoop to lift me.

Age is a window—
through its glass,
I see the history of Your presence;
the future of my hope.
Never have You left me.
Never will You forsake me.[16]

Generosity grounds me—
You have blessed me beyond measure,

10. Prov. 4:18. 11. 2 Pet. 3:13. 12. John 6:51. 13. Luke 1:53. 14. Matt. 8:12.
15. Prov. 3:6. 16. Deut. 31:6.

with every blessing in the Heavenly places.[17]
How can I not live with open arms?
Open hands?
May it be my heritage, Lord;
a legacy of love.

Resistance is my strength—
while the worldly chase after empty things,
running into ruin,
I turn my eyes to You;
I walk in the light of life.

Justice is my hope—
though sin accuses me,
You will plead my case,
nailing the record of my debt to Your cross;[18]
covering me in Your mercy.
The godless will be scattered,
while Your children join the feast.

Wisdom anchors my life—
Your words in my heart;
in my soul;
bound upon my hands;
written on my mind.[19]

When evil seeks my life,
Your truth defends me;
Your presence shields me.

Patience is a garden—
what is planted
will flourish in the fullness of time.
Though evil thrives;
the godless prosper;

17. Eph. 1:3. 18. Col. 2:14. 19. Deut. 11:18.

the wheat and weeds grow together,
the time of harvest will come.[20]

Peace is my destination—
the hope of glory:[21]
Darkness scattered.
Evil undone.
A world made new.

Salvation is my banner—
a flag,
flying full mast,
proclaiming
*"The Lord,
my Help.
Savior.
Defender.
Refuge.
Strength."*

Lord, You are Wisdom.
I sit at Your feet.
I choose the Way of Grace.

20. Matt. 13:24–30. 21. Rom. 5:2; Col. 1:27.

SHATTERED PORTRAIT

Lord,
I long to walk in Your ways[1]—
to flourish in faithfulness.
To be holy.
Set apart.
Uncompromised.

But once again,
I have failed;
fallen short of Your glory;[2]
I run after empty things
that cannot profit or deliver.[3]

Have mercy, Lord!
Though I am guilty,
do not turn a face of judgment upon me;
for who can stand before You?
Your glory is a weight I cannot bear.

Shame has made me ill;
sin's sickness saps life from me:
the consequences of my corruption.
I sink deeper into the mire;
a slow surrender.

I waste away;
pain a constant companion—
a sobering reminder that I am still alive:
a withering shell of a human;
a shattered portrait of God.

1. Deut. 10:12–13. 2. Rom. 3:22–24. 3. 1 Sam. 12:21.

I cling to the hope that I am not forgotten;
that You see and know;
that, though I plunge to the depths of the earth,
You will not forsake me.
Are You not near to the brokenhearted?[4]
A friend to the contrite in heart?[5]

I hang by a thread;
Joy and gladness are dim memories.
Even my closest friends seem miles away.
I see no hope in the land of the living.

Evil lurks in this deep darkness,
reveling in my ruin;
delighting in my destruction.

I'm in no shape to fight:
mind numb,
strength sapped,
prayers squandered.

Must the story end like this?
I have no choice but to wait,
and trust that You can find me here,
that my enemy will not have the final word.

I am prostrate before You:
sorrowful,
repentant,
painfully aware of my weakness
and my need of Your strength.

Only by Your Spirit
will I stand fast,
for my enemy prowls around like a lion,
seeking someone to devour.[6]

4. Ps. 34:18. 5. Isa. 57:15. 6. 1 Pet. 5:8.

I am reviled,
mocked,
persecuted,
for Your name's sake.

In this I am blessed.

Give me strength to resist temptation,
that the devil may flee;
to draw near to You,
that You would draw near to me.[7]
For You are my only hope
in life and death.
Amen.

7. James 4:8.

SAVED BY GRACE

Lord Jesus,
have mercy on me,
a sinner.[1]

How often have I pledged to be perfect?
To sidestep sin with quick restraint;
to barricade my heart
that iniquity might find no entry;
to walk in holiness before all,
the very embodiment of saving grace?

What a fool I have been.

For as long as I can remember,
sin has had its hooks in me.
It burns within;
a fire in my lungs—
as natural as breathing.
Regret is a constant companion;
a voice in my dreams;
a whisper as I wake.

I've lived some years upon this earth.
If You will it, I will live some more—
but I fear I have wasted so much time.
(Where does the time go?)

One day I am a child in my parents' house;
now I am grown;
now I am dying.

1. Derived from the Jesus Prayer of liturgical tradition.

My life is a word
on a page
in a book
on a shelf
in a storehouse
of books
and shelves.

What is the end of it all?

I was born in sin's grip—
a sinner,
descended from sinners;
a hereditary sickness.

What hope have I but You, Lord?
In Your mercy
You have paid my debt;
cast my failures into forgetfulness;[2]
healed my brokenness.
Your grace undeserved,
is a spring of living water.

All is not lost,
for my Redeemer lives,
and You will stand upon the earth[3]
in a world made new.

Teach me to laugh in the face of fear;
to find joy in the midst of suffering.
May I be an instrument of peace[4]
to those around me—
extending healing
to those I have harmed.

2. Mic. 7:19. 3. Job 19:25. 4. Derived from the Prayer of Saint Francis.

You are the Healer of Memories.
The Righter of Wrongs.
On this short path,
for a time,
a season,
You invite me to walk with You:
my Guide through this land of shadow.
Grant me the gift of faith
in the power of Your cross—
the Sign of Grace for me.

Lord Jesus,
have mercy on me,
a sinner,
saved by grace.

A TESTIMONY TO SALVATION

Father God,
it is a good thing to remember Your mercy;
to recall Your faithfulness in days past;
to remind myself that my very life
is a testimony to Your salvation.
For I have known the saving hand of God
after patient pleading—
when I held to Your goodness,
though Heaven was silent
and troubles increased.

I see now that Your silence was not absence;
that my desolation was not my undoing.
In Your time—
why must long-suffering be such long suffering?—
You plunged into the darkness that held me.
Raised me from ruin.
Reclaimed me.
Restored me.
Rooted and established me in love.[1]

Just when I had lost the will to sing,
Your mercy became music to me;
an old song—
older than this tired earth—
and yet, somehow,
as fresh and new as the morning.

It is not Your will that any should perish,[2]
but that all should repent
and enter into Your joy.

1. Eph. 3:16–19. 2. 2 Pet. 3:9.

It is a good thing to fall into
the hands of the Living God[3]—
to surrender to Your grace;
to trade pride for humility;
pleasant fictions for hard truths.

I am in awe of Your goodness—
that You,
Maker of all things,
would condescend to dwell with us:
the eternal Word made flesh;[4]
one with the Father;[5]
all things created through You;[6]
obedient to the point of death;[7]
triumphant in resurrection;
King of New Creation.

A Story as simple as song,
as infinite as the heavens:
of grace given;
death defeated.

Indeed, the old has passed away;
the new has come[8]—
and yet, many look for You in passing things:
in outward displays of devotion;
in rites and rituals,
practicing piety in the sight of others,
while You look at the heart.[9]

Many live in tombs of their own making,
seeking the living among the dead.[10]

But I will meet You in the secret place,
to be seen only by You,

3. Heb. 10:31. 4. John 1:14. 5. John 10:30. 6. Col. 1:16. 7. Phil. 2:8.
8. 2 Cor. 5:17. 9. 1 Sam. 16:7. 10. Luke 24:5.

as I seek to worship You in spirit and truth:[11]
a stumbler learning grace.

What a beautiful sound it is when Your family gathers;
when Your ransomed children sing the glories of Your grace;
when we feast in honor of our King.
May I never cease to join that song—
to proclaim with all the saints
the height and depth
and length and breadth
of Your love.[12]

May my words,
my thoughts,
my deepest meditations
be music to Your ears.[13]

I know You will not forsake me;[14]
that Your right hand upholds me;[15]
that Your grace is sufficient,
even for a sinner such as me.[16]

Trouble meets me at every turn.
Suffering surrounds me.
Pride blinds me.
Sin afflicts me.
What a tangled mess of contradictions I am.

But You are the great Sanctifier,
who turns deserts into springs of water;[17]
who raises the needy from affliction;
who saves all who draw near in faith.[18]

Deliver me, O Christ,
from darkness within and without—

11. John 4:23–24. 12. Rom. 8:38–39. 13. Ps. 19:14. 14. Josh. 1:5.
15. Ps. 63:8. 16. 2 Cor. 12:9. 17. Ps. 107:35. 18. Heb. 10:22.

from sin which invites
theft,
death,
and destruction.[19]

Draw me back to Your heart;
to the peace from which I so often flee.
Let Your song rise up in me again,
as I remember the grace
to which I am so great a debtor.[20]

I may be a poor excuse for a saint,
but You have made a place for me at Your table.
I may be weighed down with sorrow;
saddled with grief,
but I will rejoice at the wedding feast of the Lamb.

Come, Lord Jesus;
quickly come![21]
Amen.

19. John 10:10. 20. Inspired by the 1758 hymn "Come Thou Fount of Every Blessing" by Robert Robinson. 21. Rev. 22:20.

YOU SEE THE POOR

Lord,
You see the poor.
May I see them
as You see them;
love them
as You love them.

For You have chosen what is foolish in the world
to shame the wise;
what is weak in the world
to shame the strong.[1]

Who is like You,
a God who sides with outcasts?[2]
Dines with sinners?[3]
You were rich,
but became poor for my sake,
that through Your poverty
I might become rich.[4]

May I be one with the poor.
Near to the broken.
United in poverty of spirit before You.
For are we not all debtors in the house of God?
The one who sees the hungry,
the marginalized,
the voiceless,
sees Your face.

1. 1 Cor. 1:27. 2. Ps. 34:18. 3. Matt. 9:10; Mark 2:16; Luke 5:30. 4. 2 Cor. 8:9.

In Your kingdom,
the last are first;
the first are last;
the merciful receive mercy;[5]
the persecuted find peace;[6]
the humble of heart
are crowned with glory;[7]
blessing and honor are given
to the servant of all;
health and happiness
to the compassionate;
life abundant
to the one who loves well.

This world is filled with careless cursing.
The arrogant sneer at the suffering.
Friends betray friends.
Nothing is sacred.

You have said I will be hated for Your name's sake;[8]
in sharing Your heart,
I will share in Your suffering.
I will be mocked.
Misinterpreted.
Misunderstood.
Delivered over to death daily.[9]

Though I am not without sin—
forgive my debts,
as I have forgiven my debtors[10]—
they wrongfully accuse me,
twisting my words.

But You see the heart.

---

5. Matt. 5:7. 6. Matt 5:10. 7. Matt. 18:4. 8. Matt. 10:22. 9. 2 Cor. 4:11.
10. Matt. 6:12.

God forbid I should speak without compassion.
Save me from casual blasphemy;
from pride's
gutting
gorging
gravity.

I will not be forsaken.
Struck down.
Destroyed.[11]
Your life will be manifested in me.[12]
I will rise again,
to walk with You
in the mission of mercy:
saved by grace,
that I might show grace to others;
blessed,
that I might be a blessing.

Lord,
You see the poor.
May I see them
as You see them;
love them
as You love them;
for what I do to the least of these
I do to You.[13]

11. 2 Cor. 4:9. 12. 2 Cor. 4:10. 13. Matt. 25:40.

SEIZED BY LONGING

Father God,
there is a hunger only You can satisfy;
a thirst only You can quench;[1]
a yearning unfulfilled until You meet it.
I have known the comfort of Your hand upon me;
the fellowship of Your presence with me.
But now there is only silence—
a void where Your Spirit once was pleased to dwell.

I close my eyes
and I'm standing at the river's edge.
I turn, and see—
a deer crouched over the current;
tongue lapping at the water,
slaking its thirst.
Seized by longing,
I kneel to drink,
and the dream ends.

How long will this longing last?
How deep is the darkness that binds me?
I have wept and pleaded,
suffering this soul-sickness:
the absence of a God
some say was never there to begin with.

But I know better.
There were days when You were close enough to touch;
when I stood upon mountains
and looked into the face of God.

1. Ps. 107:9.

I have met You in the gathering of the saints—
in bread and wine;
in song and celebration.

Meet me again, Lord.

May the peace of God
guard my heart and mind,[2]
bringing rest to unrest;
consolation to desolation;
as I cling to His promises,[3]
as sure of their coming
as the rising of the sun.

All about me is darkness;
I see no end to this struggle.
But I know that the dark is light to You,[4]
depth is height to You.
Have You ever truly left me, Lord?
Could You?
You, who fill all things?
I seek solace in peaceful waters,
but the ripple becomes a current;
becomes a raging sea.
I am lost in the swells.

Are You not here as well, Lord?
You, who brooded over the waters?[5]
All creation testifies to Your kindness:
waning moons and rising suns—
daily resurrection.
Even in despair,
I remember and proclaim:
this darkness will not win;
all nights end.

2. Phil. 4:7. 3. 2 Pet. 1:4. 4. Ps. 139:11–12. 5. Gen. 1:2.

Why do You hide Yourself?
Do You hide,
that I would seek?
Withdraw,
that I would follow?
Is there logic to this longing?
Purpose to this pain?
I am haunted by devils—
a chorus of crooked voices:
lost, they call me.
Never saved.
Never loved.
Never comforted.

May the peace of God
guard my heart and mind,[6]
bringing rest to unrest;
consolation to desolation;
as I cling to His promises,[7]
as sure of their coming
as the rising of the sun.

6. Phil. 4:7. 7. 2 Pet. 1:4.

CHRIST WHO SAVES

Christ Who Saves,[1]
I seek shelter in You once again.
Evil chases me in a godless land—
wind and rain thrashing about me,
the sky a starless void,
groaning and shrieking
as the earth gives way beneath me.

Be a window in the darkness, Lord—
hearth-lit in the distance;
a haven in this hell.

For I see no hope of escape.
I am weighed down with worry:
broken;
burdened;
shouldering this grief alone.

Where are You, Lord?

Be my beacon—
a light in this endless night.
Guide me to higher ground;[2]
to the shelter of Your presence;
a refuge in the storm.[3]

Praise and adoration will flow out of me;
songs of joy and thanksgiving—
for You are the Deliverer of my soul,
and in Your arms I find rest.

1. Ps. 68:20. 2. Ps. 61:2. 3. Isa. 25:4.

Speak to my heart:
"Do not be low-eyed;
heavy-laden;
ground-scavenging for help.
Lift your gaze;
turn your eyes upon Me,
for there is hope for you yet."

You will not depart from me;[4]
my future is in Your hands—
the spring of all my joy and peace;
the Christ Who Saves.

4. Deut. 31:6.

BROKEN FAMILY

Father,
for as long as I can remember,
Your words have been my bread[1]—
Sustaining Story
handed down,
generation to generation;
the annals of Your faithfulness.

Like a shepherd,
You led Israel,[2]
planting them in a fruitful land
of hills and valleys
drinking rain from Heaven.[3]
Not by human strength
did they conquer their foes,
but by Your mercy and might alone.[4]
You worked wonders among them,
tabernacling in cloud and fire[5]—
a present God.

Through the miracle of grace,
I am grafted into Your family:[6]
ransomed with blood;[7]
raised with Christ.[8]
With all the saints I pray,
may Your kingdom come;[9]
may darkness fall;
may every enemy be destroyed

1. Matt. 4:4. 2. Jer. 31:10. 3. Deut. 11:11. 4. Ps. 20:7. 5. Exod. 13:21.
6. Rom. 11:17. 7. 1 Pet. 1:18–19. 8. Col. 3:1; Eph. 2:5–6. 9. Matt. 6:10;
Luke 11:12.

until death dies[10]
and New Creation reigns.

I put little faith in human strength—
in the march of progress;
the worldly boasting of bright tomorrows.
My hope is in You,
and You alone:
King of all the earth;
the One who brings life from death;
peace from peril;
good from evil.[11]

Be praised, Lord,
for all You have done.
Salvation belongs to You,[12]
and You give it to all who come.
For this,
and for all Your many mercies,
I will lift my voice in praise.

But in these difficult days,
You have grown silent.
The power of Your Spirit has withdrawn.
Your Church has grown cold and lifeless.
Faith has withered.
Miracles are in short supply.

We are a broken family,
dominated by division—
known not for our love,
but for our loathing.
We have traded humility for power;
truth for relevance;
the sufferings of Christ for the comforts of Babylon.

10. 1 Cor. 15:26. 11. Gen. 50:20. 12. Ps. 3:8.

And so we have lost our right to speak;
to proclaim;
to judge.
We are a crude joke in the mouth of the world;
a pale shadow of Your triumphant Bride;
a chosen people wandering in the wilderness.

We are dismantled,
piece by piece;
cathedrals dismembered
and sold as scraps.
How long will You stand by,
watching this slow death?
Will You allow us to destroy ourselves
in Your name?

It is a burden on my back;
a grief I carry in my bones:
the glory of God lies dormant
and our witness withers.

I am ashamed—
not of You
or Your grace
or Your truth—
but of what we have become:
loveless.
lifeless.
lukewarm.

And yet, Lord,
and yet:
there are many who remain faithful;
who cling to You
when others stray;

who stand on Your promises
when others wander;
who consider the reproach of Christ
greater wealth than the treasures of Egypt.[13]

May I be counted among them—
one who fans into flame the gift of God[14]
when all around grows cold;
who remains steadfast under trial;[15]
who conquers by the blood of the Lamb
and the word of my testimony.[16]

May it be so, Lord.

But the grief remains.
When will You restore the glory of Your house?[17]
When will this fractured family
become Your radiant Bride?
Turn Your face upon us;
have mercy on us;
that these dry bones might live again.[18]
Save us from ourselves,
so that we might once again
walk as the beloved of God,
in the power of God,
to the glory of Your name.
Amen.

13. Heb. 11:26. 14. 2 Tim. 1:6. 15. James 1:12. 16. Rev. 12:11. 17. Ps. 26:8.
18. Ezek. 37:3.

IN UNION

Love is a song in my heart—
a song You first sang to me;
a swelling,
soaring,
symphony of sound—
a river swollen by Winter,
released in Spring;
a cup running over;[1]
an uncontainable flood.

I am Your beloved:
Betrothed.
Bound to You
in everlasting union.

You forsook beauty;
majesty;[2]
power;
to be pierced for my transgressions;
crushed for my iniquities;[3]
to bear the curse of the cross;[4]
learning obedience through Your suffering,[5]
that I—
unable to save myself—
might be redeemed;
restored;
raised to new life.[6]

Dominion is Yours;
Your kingdom everlasting;[7]

1. Ps. 23:5. 2. Isa. 53:2. 3. Isa. 53:5. 4. Gal. 3:13. 5. Heb. 5:8. 6. Rom. 6:4.
7. Ps. 135:13.

Your government and peace
will know no end.[8]

Therefore You are exalted:
King of all the earth;
the One to whom every knee will bow,
every tongue confess Your lordship.[9]
You have brought a sword upon the earth,
piercing through soul and spirit,
joint and marrow.[10]
Who can stand before You
but those who have entered Your joy?

I have counted everything as loss
for the surpassing worth
of knowing You, my Lord.[11]
Old ways have been forgotten.
Old paths forsaken.
I was bedridden with regret;
lost in hopeless fear;
until You breathed new life into me.
With gentleness,
You healed my brokenness,
restoring years
stolen by fear and worry.

You have arrayed me
in Truth.
Righteousness.
Readiness.
Guarded me with Faith.
Salvation.
The Sword of Your Spirit.[12]

8. Isa. 9:7.   9. Phil. 2:9–11.   10. Heb. 4:12.   11. Phil. 3:8.   12. Eph. 6:13–17.

I wake in the house of God,
at peace in Your presence,
each day a new adventure
in trusting You.

Many will come from east and west
to join Your feast, O Lord,[13]
that Your house might be full;[14]
our joy complete.

What wondrous love,[15]
to be called children of God:[16]
Beloved.
Betrothed.
Bound to You
in everlasting union.[17]

13. Matt. 8:11. 14. Luke 14:23. 15. From the folk hymn "What Wondrous Love Is This." 16. 1 John 3:1. 17. 1 John 4:13.

THE ONE SAFE PLACE

Father God,
You are the One Safe Place—
the only abiding Shelter
in this windswept world;
North Star in ink-black night.
Constant in variable.
Just and rightful Ruler
in a land of cardboard kingdoms.

If all nature withers;
all strong things break—
hills become valleys;
seas tip like a cup
to flood the fractured earth—
if all hell breaks loose
to wind its cord of chaos
around the neck of the world,
You will remain—
arms outstretched
in posture of embrace,
to reconcile all things to Yourself.[1]
All shattered pieces of time and space:
Restored.
Confirmed.
Strengthened.
Established.[2]

And so You will build a city:
radiant,
like a bride;

1. Col. 1:20. 2. 1 Pet. 5:10.

Citadel of All Things New.
You will be its light and laughter;
the joyful Lord of New Creation!
Your river—
bright as crystal,
wending through its streets.
Your tree—
seed of Eden,
promising healing
to all who come
from far-flung corners of creation
to Your ever-open City.[3]

The kingdoms of earth are two-bit theater;
the roles ever-changing—
grown men playing at conquest
until death resets the scene.

One breath from Your mouth;
a single word from the One True King—
and the great dominion of humanity
is reduced to nothing.

In the end,
only one kingdom will stand;
one King reign.
In Your mercy
You will preserve and protect me.
I will see dawn break
on the great and terrible day of the Lord,
when You come with vengeance
and the awful might of Your mercy—
to disarm darkness;
scatter sorrow;
peel the veil of death from the world.

3. Rev. 22:1–2.

You will not rest until all wars have ceased;
all evil is vanquished;
all tyranny forgotten.

Help me, Father,
to find a corner of quiet in the storm;
to find You in that sacred silence
and remember who You are:
King.
Lord.
God with us.
Preserver.
Protector.
Amen.

BLESSED TRINITY

Blessed Trinity!
My heart resounds with thankful praise;
a joyous clamor;
a grave-shaking racket;
songs to wake the dead.

Deep respect,
honor,
reverence
shape my praise—
High God of Heaven:
Father.
Son.
Spirit.

You rule and reign
over every throne,
dominion,
power upon the earth.[1]
You carve paths through the wilderness
for the faithful,
fighting battles on our behalf;[2]
leading us to a place of abundance:
Holy Ground,
wholly given.

Songs well up in me—
I can't help but sing Your mercy;
voice Your grace.

1. Col. 1:16. 2. 2 Chron. 20:17.

There is none like You
in Heaven
or on earth:
keeping covenant;
showing steadfast love.[3]

All who love You
will gather at Your everlasting feast,
clothed in Your mercy;
held by Your love.

All powers
are Your possession;
all allegiance belongs to You:
Father.
Son.
Spirit.
Blessed Trinity!

3. 1 Kings 8:23.

KING OF NEW JERUSALEM

Lord God,
give me a heart that longs for New Creation;
that clings to the promise of that blessed Not Yet.
Here, in this land of shade and shadow,
all grows old and grey,
lost to the hands of time.

I look to the City that is to come.

In that eternal dawn,
when the last enemy has been destroyed,[1]
You will be glorified, Lord—
the rightful Ruler of a world made new:
the King of New Jerusalem.

How I long to see that City:
enthroned upon the earth;
the whispered wonder of the world;
the place where God dwells with us;[2]
where sighing and sorrow flee away.

You will end all wars, Lord;
for when the kingdoms of the world mount their attack,
countless in number,
armed with every instrument of death,
they will stand in awe at the glory of Your City—
the joy of your people—
and there will be no breath left in them.

The enemies of God will be scattered;
crushed;
forgotten;

1. 1 Cor. 15:26. 2. Rev. 21:3.

at last, the long history of bloodshed upon the earth
will come to an end.

As Your people gather
to sing the glories of Your name,
sharing bread and wine
in remembrance of Your death,
may we also remember Your resurrection;
the hope of New Creation;
the mystery of Your purpose, plan, and will,
to unite all things in Christ,
things in Heaven and on earth.[3]

All Your ways are good
and worthy of praise:
Your justice merciful;
Your mercy just.
I join the assembly of the saints,
proclaiming, *"Yes and amen."*

You have preserved the holy city of Israel;
like a phoenix,
Jerusalem has risen from the ashes,
surviving siege and storm.
It suffers violence,
within and without,
yet stands—
a signpost in the mist,
pointing to a City yet to come.[4]

May I never cease to tell Your Story—
the Story of fallen humanity;
Merciful God;
Abiding Hope.
What You have begun
You will be faithful to finish.
Amen.

3. Eph. 1:10. 4. Inspired by a phrase from N. T. Wright, *Surprised by Hope* (New York: HarperOne, 2008), 132.

YOUR TRUTH

Lord,
in these difficult days,
truth is in short supply—
one voice among many
in a murmuring marketplace
of soap-box preachers;
vendors peddling
the various Gospels of the Now.

May I have the courage
to speak Your Truth:
Word-wed Wisdom
in an age of empty promises.
May my heart be a place of quiet meditation,
Your steadfast love
and faithfulness
inscribed upon it.[1]

May I lean full-tilt into Your embrace,
rooted and grounded in love.[2]
Speak to me, God—
in words ancient as the earth
and fresh as the dawn—
Truth untroubled by time;
a song sung by the stars;
proclaimed by earth and Heaven.
May I join in that eternal chorus,
and in my own way

1. Prov. 3:3. 2. Eph. 3:17.

set it to sound;
to tone;
to flame.

Why do I walk the world afraid
when You are with me?
Why do I fear the lies of the lost
when You are a shield around me?[3]
Why do I grieve when the wicked prosper;
when none can buy their way out of the grave?
The best of us;
the worst of us,
suffer the same fate:
death comes for us all.

The path is riddled with pain
for all who resist You;
who walk in bondage
and call it liberty;
who worship self
and call it freedom.
They wander in trackless wastes,
building homes in shifting sand;
in the land of dead and dying things.

As for me,
I will see You, Lord.
Though my flesh is destroyed
and my body wastes away,[4]
I know You will stand again upon the earth,[5]
and in the twinkling of an eye,
I will be changed.[6]

Tune my ears to hear Your voice
above the noise and clamor;

3. 2 Sam. 22:31; Ps. 18:30; 119:114; Prov. 30:5. 4. Job 19:26. 5. Job 19:25.
6. 1 Cor. 15:52.

the busy chattering of the dead.
Without You,
our wisdom is folly;
our knowledge is vain.

GROUNDED BY GRATITUDE

Father God,
You are King of all things
and sustain all things with the word of Your power.[1]
You are Earth-Whisperer;
Moon-Marshaller;
Sun-Summoner;
Fountain of truth
and beauty
and wisdom.
Your light shines,
and the darkness has not overcome it.[2]

By no means are You silent or removed;
You have made Yourself known,
and made us to know You.
You rule in fearsome majesty,
clothed in a hurricane of fire,
wielding a sword of justice
and a heart of mercy.
Like a bridegroom You call,
"Come to me,
all who are washed in the blood of the Lamb—
come to the marriage feast!"[3]

You discipline the ones You love,[4]
rebuking our faithlessness;
condemning our empty praise.
We are outwardly righteous;
inwardly lawless;[5]
we have forgotten the meaning of sacrifice.

1. Heb. 1:3. 2. John 1:5. 3. Rev. 19:9. 4. Heb. 12:6. 5. Matt. 23:28.

What can we give You, Lord,
when earth and Heaven are Yours,[6]
and all things Your rightful possession?
What gift can we bring
when every good gift is from Your hands?[7]

Can we give You silver or gold,
when You have arrayed us in the righteousness of Christ?[8]
Can we give You offerings of blood,
when Christ has been sacrificed once and for all?[9]

A repentant heart,
thanks overflowing,
is the best we can bring—
a confident leaning upon grace;
a settled trust in Your faithfulness.

There are many who mock Your mercy,
twisting Your words in derision—
conceit-swollen;
pleasure-lovers;[10]
insatiable in their sin.
They curse carelessly,
dragging others into darkness,
forgetting that life and death are in the power of the tongue.[11]

For a time You have overlooked their ignorance,
but now all are called to repent;
for the risen Christ will judge the world.[12]

May they seek You while You may be found;
call upon You while You are near;[13]
before evil days come.[14]

6. Deut. 10:14; Ps. 24:1; 89:11. 7. James 1:17. 8. Gal. 3:27. 9. Heb. 10:10.
10. 2 Tim. 3:4. 11. Prov. 18:21. 12. Acts 17:30–31. 13. Isa. 55:6.
14. Eccles. 12:1.

You are not slow to fulfill Your promises,
but are patient,
desiring all to come to a knowledge of the truth.[15]

Blessed are those who are grounded by gratitude;
who live as happy debtors to grace;[16]
who worship You in spirit and in truth;[17]
for theirs is the Kingdom of Heaven.

15. 2 Pet. 3:9. 16. Rom. 8:12. 17. John 4:23.

RESTORER
OF BROKEN THINGS

Gracious Lord,
I come before You today,
burdened with sin;
desperate for the mercy only You can show—
not as a result of anything I have done,[1]
but because You are infinitely good:
the Restorer of Broken Things.

Only by Your grace
can the death grip of my sin be
unraveled,
unyoked,
undone.
Shower me in Your mercy, Lord;
cleanse me of all that is unholy,
unhealthy,
unworthy.

I walk with wayward feet,
drawn by godless gravity:
a constant reminder of all I have done
and left undone.[2]
Does not all goodness flow from You?
Is not every transgression,
every step toward darkness,

1. 2 Tim. 1:9. 2. Episcopal Church, *The Book of Common Prayer and Administration of the Sacraments and Other Rites and Ceremonies of the Church* (New York: Oxford University Press, 1990), 360.

a sin against You
and You alone?
Only You are worthy to judge.

From the moment I was born,
I was painted with sin's brush.
From my first breath,
I've been bent deathwards.

You rebuild the house of my heart—
attic to basement;
every part of me revealed,
redeemed,
restored.
In painful discipline
You shape me,
form me,
yielding the peaceful fruit of righteousness.[3]

Wash me, Lord.[4]
Let it be as though those
dark and dreadful things
never happened.
Help me remember
that You are God of the Feast;
that joy and gladness can lift a heavy heart.

Open my soul to levity and laughter;
to the Good News that makes the lame dance,
the blind see,
the captive free.[5]

In Your mercy,
forget what I've been;
purge it from Your memory.

3. Heb. 12:11. 4. 1 Cor. 6:11. 5. Luke 4:16–21.

Melt this heart of stone,[6]
that I might start fresh,
from the ground up.

Whatever You do,
do not leave me;
forsake me;
distance me
from Your presence.
Do what You do best:
Renew.
Revive.
Lift me from the dust.

When I have risen,
I will tell of Your kindness,
that those who are lost in darkness
might taste and see
the goodness of God.[7]

Render an innocent verdict over me,
for You are my only hope.
You are the song of praise on my lips;
a Story that seems too good to be true,
and yet . . .
and yet . . .

You are not looking for posturing
or perfect records;
You're after those
who know when to get on their knees;
who know their own weakness;
know they are undeserving of Your mercy,
and utterly dependent upon it.

Continue Your work of redemption, Lord.

6. Ezek. 36:26. 7. Ps. 34:8.

Bring to bear the fruit of Your kingdom—
for in that new world,
all will know You
and praise You
as You rightly deserve.
Amen.

HOW LONG?

Lord God,
this world is sick with wayward love:
faithfulness mocked;
sin celebrated.
All the while, You knock,[1]
Your grace undiminished.

Many have called beauty ugliness;
ugliness, beauty;[2]
sprinting after every lust
of eye and flesh;
engorged with the pride of life;[3]
quick to sin,
slow to repent;
clinging to curses:
a vulgar benediction.

Lord,
You who desire all to come to salvation,
tell me:
How long will evil have its way?

Soon You will come—
come, Lord Jesus[4]—
soon and very soon.
How long, O Lord?
Soon, with winnowing fork in hand,
to gather the wheat;
to burn the chaff;[5]

1. Rev. 3:20. 2. Isa. 5:20. 3. 1 John 2:16. 4. Rev. 22:20. 5. Matt. 3:12.

to shatter the idols of earth,
grinding them to dust;
to grant to all their deepest desire.

In that day,
the redeemed of the Lord
will rejoice at Your judgment;
for it is a good and righteous thing
that sin be vanquished;
oppression silenced;
that evil suffers Your absence.

As for me,
may I remain in Your love,[6]
rooted and grounded in You:[7]
vine to branch;
root to soil;
producing the patient fruit of faithfulness;
having strength to comprehend with all the saints[8]
the circumference of Your goodness and grace.

May gratitude be the song on my lips;
New Creation the hope of my heart;
as Your children proclaim
the glories of Your name.
Amen.

6. John 15:9–10. 7. Eph. 3:16–19. 8. Eph. 3:17–18.

ANY ONE OF US

Lord Jesus,
bearer of God's face to all,
what a tragedy
that we—
breathed into being,
made in Your image—
should be so quick to forget You.

We are sick from the womb;
a tangle of contradictions:
crooked.
pride-poisoned.
death-bent.

Even the kinship of covenant
cannot keep us from
wavering.
wandering.
withering.
Will any one of us be fit
for the glory ahead?

We breed ignorance,
giving ourselves over to a slow death;
a four-course feast for evil.
In Your mercy,
scatter this deep darkness!
Strike its messengers
with fear and blindness!
Save us from the gut of the grave.

For we are not without hope.
Where sin reigned in death,
grace reigns through righteousness.[1]
Once we were distant,
but now we have been brought near
by Your blood,[2]
that we might walk in newness of life.[3]

How I need that life, Lord—
to breathe with fresh lungs;
to walk with renewed strength.[4]

Reach out from Your Holy Dwelling;
bring me back
to hallowed ground;
that I,
with all sin-struggling,
God-wrestling saints,
may sing the glories of Your grace.

1. Rom. 5:21. 2. Eph. 2:13. 3. Rom. 6:4. 4. Isa. 40:31.

LIVING SACRIFICE

Christ,
in Your mercy,
hear me.
In Your power,
deliver me.
In my darkest hour,
may hope lift me;
may peace,
surpassing understanding,
guard my heart and mind.[1]

I've become a target for godless gossip;
prey in the hands of the lost.
Lying voices surround me,
dealing death at every turn;
such are the times I live in.

While all around me
grasp at passing things,
I will remain steadfast, Lord;[2]
secure in Your promises;
for You are the firm foundation of my life—
my Strength.
my Song.[3]
my Confidence.

You will execute justice in the earth.
All who mock Your mercy
will suffer the absence of it;
for You are a consuming fire.[4]

1. Phil. 4:6–7. 2. Ps. 108:1. 3. Exod. 15:2. 4. Heb. 12:28–29.

May my life be a living sacrifice;[5]
my heart an altar of praise;
for You have redeemed me from the grave;[6]
lifted me to new life;
delivered me from evil.[7]

5. Rom. 12:1. 6. Ps. 103:2–5. 7. Matt. 6:13.

OPEN HEART

———————

Listening Lord,
listen now.
Speaking God,
speak to me now.
I am crushed by fear,
weighed down with worry,
with no sign of relief in sight.

I am heart-sick;
death-dreading;
flung into a nightmare world.
Hunted.
Hounded.
Lost in a labyrinth of death.

If I could fly away, Lord;
make for the skies like a bird;
I'd be off in a moment—
off to some far-flung Heaven
beyond the reach of this hell.

Here I am,
dreaming of escape
while cities burn;
the innocent suffer;
as evil spins its web
around the world—
an encircling darkness;
a pall over every living thing.

———————

The worst wounds of all
come at the hands of friends.
One might hide from enemies,
but friends find you.
Once, we walked together—
blessing You;
revering You;
beholding Your glory;
knit together by grace—
until betrayal loosed the thread,
and their faces were turned away from me.

Surely they are storing up wrath for themselves.[1]
Surely such wanton treachery;
such ungodliness,
unrighteousness,[2]
only invites death.

As for me,
in all my struggles
I have learned this to be true:
from the waking of the day
to its slumber,
I am heard by You.
Seen by You.

Out of the abundance of Your love,
You deliver me from darkness;
surround me in conflict;
uphold my cause.
I will live to see the humbling of the proud;
the gutting of the godless.
They will fall along the wide path
that leads to destruction.[3]

1. Rom. 2:5. 2. Rom. 1:18. 3. Matt. 7:13.

A Judas kiss is a wound like no other.
With flattering phrases
he soothes and subdues,
all the while sharpening his blade for the kill;
a traitor's words are a dagger to the heart.

In distress,
I open my heart to You, Lord.
I pour out its treasure
into Your open hands—
until fear subsides
and my spirit rests.

I take comfort in the knowledge
that this suffering will one day end;
that evil will not have the final word.

Come quickly, Lord Jesus.[4]
All my hope is in You.

4. Rev. 22:20.

WHEN STRENGTH FAILS

Christ, have mercy.
There are days when the whole world seems turned
against me;
when every stranger is an enemy;
every word a lie;
every glance a threat.
I am attacked on all sides—
battered;
boot-struck;
heaved face-first into the gutter.

When dread grips my heart;
when my strength fails;
may I remember Your faithfulness.
Recall Your kindness.
Cling to Your goodness.

I am a child of God,
Maker of Heaven and Earth;
what power does fear have over me?

The dawn brings new threats;
fresh terrors to endure;
as the voices of derision multiply:
a widespread worship of wind.

How does one walk with You in such a godless place?
When Your law is mocked in every street;
Your name torn from every page?[1]
They despise Your way

1. Jer. 36:21–24.

and all who walk in it.
All who refuse to join them
become their sworn enemies.
They bait and trap them,
condemning them
while they hold fast to evil and call it good.[2]
All the while,
they store up wrath for themselves,
for You will return to judge the living and the dead.[3]

As for me,
I have suffered,
but not in vain.
You have walked with me in my weakness;
met me in my mourning;
through Your grace I have persevered;
endured;
hoped.[4]
One day, these sorrows will subside;
this languishing will end;
when You swallow death
and wipe these tears away.[5]

Never have You left me.
Never have I been forsaken.[6]
Though dread grips me;
though strength fails me;
I remember
Your faithfulness.
Your kindness.
Your goodness.

I am a child of God,
Maker of Heaven and Earth;
what power does fear have over me?

2. Isa. 5:20. 3. 1 Pet. 4:5. 4. Rom. 5:3–4. 5. Isa. 25:7–8. 6. Ps. 37:25.

I am broken,
but I will praise You.
I am given over to death for Your sake,
that Your life may be manifested in me[7]
as I share in Your sufferings[8]
and in Your comfort,
until all is made new.
Amen.

7. 2 Cor. 4:11. 8. 2 Cor. 1:5.

THESE RIVAL POWERS

Lord Almighty,
present and powerful,
I come to You for mercy
in this hour,
this time,
in which I live.
I am wind-battered;
cross-pressured;
desperate for some reprieve.

There are powers in this world
that desire our devotion.
By eloquence
and influence
they gain ground:
a widespread idolatry.
They steal into homes,
into hearts;
mimicking Your beauty,
Your creativity,
Your power;
impersonating Your goodness,
Your kingship,
Your reign;
pledging peace,
freedom,
justice.
With empty promises,
they seek my soul's allegiance.

Darkness circles me,
ravenous with hunger.
I am
Cornered.
Captured.
Easy prey.

Rise to protect me, Lord!
Shield me from the fangs of death.
Hide me in Your arms;
defend my cause.

Be praised!
Be honored!
Be lifted high in the earth!
May all forces of evil
be put to flight.
May they trip into snares
of their own making.
Save me, Lord,
from the sway of lesser gods—
from any pledge,
promise,
paradigm
that turns my eyes from You.

May faith arise in me.
May words of blessing,
acclaim,
adoration
flow from my heart—
a song of thankful praise to You:
Mighty God.
Eternal Father.[1]
King of Creation.

1. Isa. 9:6.

Your mercy is unmatchable.
Your love inimitable.
Your kingdom unstoppable.

PSALM 58

MARKETPLACE OF IDOLS

Lord,
this world is a marketplace of idols,[1]
wayward worship at every turn—
false gods promising peace;
paths promising righteousness,
but leading to death.[2]

We are born to trouble
as the sparks fly upwards.[3]
Unchecked, we flee from Your presence,
clothing ourselves in lies:[4]
a cursed covering.
You call out in the cool of the day,[5]
but many wander out of earshot,
suppressing the truth,
seeking their own wisdom;
becoming fools;
exchanging Your glory
for passing things.[6]

Their own works will condemn them,[7]
when You once again appear
to judge the living and the dead.[8]
In that day,
their strength will be broken;
their confidence will melt away within them
when they look upon the ruin of their rule;
the desolation of their domain.

1. Acts 17:16. 2. Prov. 14:12. 3. Job 5:7. 4. Gen. 3:7. 5. Gen. 3:8.
6. Rom. 1:22–23. 7. Rev. 20:12. 8. 1 Pet. 4:5.

They will wish they had never been born;
had never emerged from the womb;
but had remained
un-formed.
un-made.
un-spirited.
Such are those who blaspheme Your Spirit;[9]
they become what they worship.

The children of God—
all who gather at Your marriage supper[10]—
will lift their voices in praise,
for Your judgments are true and just.[11]
You have conquered death;
overthrown evil;
Ascended Lord,
Judge of the Earth.[12]

9. Mark 3:29; Luke 12:10. 10. Rev. 19:6–10. 11. Rev. 19:1–2.
12. Acts 2:33.

DELIVER ME FROM EVIL

Jesus,
my Savior,
deliver me from evil.[1]

Though I have walked in the way of Life,[2]
keeping to Your paths,
my eyes fixed upon You,
evil pursues me;
sin afflicts me—
darkness within and without;
the power of the air[3]
and my own judgments and jealousies
seek to poison my mind;
mutate my motives—
a persistent threat;
a present danger.

Faith is a waiting game;
patient expectation
in the midst of crippling fear
and sleepless nights.
Often I feel like a lamb
led to the slaughter;
a sheep flung among wolves.[4]

Deliver me, Lord.
Wage war on my behalf.
As a lion defends its young,
bare Your holy arm[5]
in the sight of my foes.

1. Matt. 6:13. 2. John 14:6. 3. Eph. 2:2. 4. Matt. 10:16; Luke 10:3.
5. Isa. 52:10.

Fall upon them when they circle me,
counting my bones;[6]
do not let them escape.

May we laugh together
when evil is overthrown;
when darkness is scattered;
when all that is hidden comes to light.
From the shelter of Your arms
I will watch as dawn breaks
in a world made new.

Jesus,
my Savior,
deliver me from evil.

Have You not proven Yourself
time and time again to be
Lord?
Liberator?
Lover?

Grant me victory,
and may it be a testimony to all
that none can stand against You—
that no trial,
tribulation,
danger,
sword
can separate me from Your love.[7]

Sin sang to me,
but Your song was louder still.
The howling hunger of death pursed me,
but I had food from Heaven:[8]

6. Ps. 22:17. 7. Rom. 8:39. 8. John 4:32.

Your body, my meal;
Your blood, my cup.

We have wrestled, You and I;
limbs twisted until daybreak.[9]
By Your mercy,
I limp my way to kingdom come.

Jesus,
my Savior,
deliver me from evil.

9. Gen. 32:24.

REBUILDER OF RUINS

Lord Jesus,
my heart grieves for the people of God.
Your Church—
founded to be a light to the world;
a city on a hill[1]—
is a pale shadow of its former self:
its foundations broken;
its stones shattered.
Is this the hand of Your judgment upon us?
Has Your Spirit withdrawn?
Your glory departed?

Our eyes have been opened to our faithlessness.
We are known for our hypocrisy;
famous for our failings:
a bitter pill to swallow.

But there are some who love You still;
who would trade wealth and influence
for poverty in Your presence;
who still believe You are the only hope of this world—
a standard in the wilderness—
that whoever believes in You
might have eternal life.[2]
Remember, Lord;
remember those who love You still.

In the latter days,
Your city will be established in the earth;
the highest of the mountains;

1. Matt. 5:14. 2. John 3:14–15.

and the nations will flow to it.[3]
You will restore the fortunes of Your people;
Your children will know peace at last;
and our joy will be complete.[4]

I believe it, Lord—
but when?
When will this weight of sorrow be lifted?
When will this long affliction end?
When will Your Church be filled with glory once again?

Only by Your strength
will we overcome.
Only by Your power
will we walk in victory.
For You are the God of Second Chances;
the Rebuilder of Ruins.[5]

3. Isa. 2:2; Mic. 4:1–2. 4. John 15:11. 5. Isa. 61:4.

JOURNEY HOME

Lord,
I know You hear the cries of my heart—
whisper to wail;
from deepest dark
to highest mountain—
You are faithful to hear me
when I reach for You,
heavy with need;
desperate for steady ground.

Long have I carried this weight—
a burden on my back,
heaved through forest
and field;
wind
and rain.
I am a wanderer upon the earth;
an exile
on a long journey home.

I have no lasting city here;[1]
no place to lay my head.[2]
What homeland have I but You?
You are a citadel in a desert waste;
a mountain island in a violent sea;
a cleft in a rock as the storm passes.
The One Safe Place.

How many times have You saved me?
Spared me?

1. Heb. 13:14. 2. Matt. 8:20; Luke 9:58.

Wrestled me from the mouth of the abyss?
With gentleness, You have
Sheltered me.
Restored me.
Given me a wide space to stand.[3]
Time and time again,
I have found myself caught
in Your relentless gravity;
an easterly wind,
blowing homeward.

Love burned within me,
a longing no lust could lift;
no sin could satisfy.
I turned my heart to You—
though You seemed so far away—
and with each feeble oath
and fragile vow,
faith began to rise—
a ripple,
a current,
a wave—
lifting me.
I was swept up in the arms of grace,
one with all the saints before me.

I am a citizen of Heaven;
a servant of the Most High King,
who reigns forever.
His kingdom an everlasting kingdom;
His government
and peace unending.[4]

By Your grace,
may this wandering end.

3. 2 Sam. 22:37; Pss. 18:36; 119:45. 4. Isa. 9:7.

With love and faithfulness,[5]
guide me homeward—
out of exile;
from fear,
famine,
death,
darkness—
into the sanctuary of Your presence.

5. Ps. 85:10.

PSALM 62

QUIET WHISPER

Lord,
teach me the sacred art of patience—
to slow mind,
body,
spirit
in the peaceful pursuit of Your presence.

Meet me, I pray, in these small hours—
with door latched;
labor deferred.
This pocket of silence
is a Remembering Place,
where You,
with gentle flame,
renew and restore me.

Great are You, Lord—
Savior.
Sustainer.
Deliverer.

*Many look for You in wind,
earthquake,
fire—
but I have learned to wait
for the quiet whisper of God.*[1]

Beyond this place
the world will press in like a vice,
my every weakness exposed;

1. 1 Kings 19:11–12.

thorns twisting into my side;
voices accusing me,
weaving a web of lies,
wreaking eloquent destruction.

I return again and again
to the comfort of Your arms.
You are the steady ground beneath my feet;[2]
the firm foundation of my heart.
There is no other
Savior.
Sustainer.
Deliverer.

Though many look for You in wind,
earthquake,
fire—
I have learned to wait
for the quiet whisper of God.[3]

May all Your people know You
in spirit and truth;[4]
in quiet intimacy;
laying all before You,
naked in their need.

We are all debtors to grace[5]—
rich and poor alike.
So much effort is wasted
in the pursuit of passing things.
In status and privilege.
In momentary increase.
A flush of pleasure.
A few minutes of fame.

2. Ps. 18:36. 3. 1 Kings 19:11–12. 4. John 4:23–24. 5. Rom. 8:12.

We look for You in earthly treasures,
in vaults assailed by moth and rust[6]—
honest or dishonest gain.

Again and again,
You guide me back to the same truth:
everything is Yours, Lord[7]—
all that I am,
all that I have,
is a gift from Your hand.[8]
In plenty or in hunger;
in abundance or need;
I have mastered contentment,[9]
for You are with me.

May I journey deeper still
into the heart of God,
desiring You above all things;[10]
for You reward the patient seeker.
You satisfy the longing soul.
Whether we are drawn in or cast out—
the choice is ours.

6. Matt. 6:19. 7. Ps. 24:1. 8. 1 Chron. 29:14. 9. Phil. 4:11. 10. Ps. 73:25.

GOOD AND SUSTAINING GOD

Good and Sustaining God,
who first chose me,[1]
You are the treasure I seek[2]—
the end of all my longings;
a thirst I cannot quench;
an ever-present hunger—
I, a beggar at the door of grace.

What mountains we have stood upon together—
my soul swept up in a cloud of glory;
the heavens opened
as I beheld Your face—
a distant memory now;
a vague recollection.

Still, I would rather face death—
disappear from this world,
be utterly forgotten—
than suffer separation from You.
The dim glory of the past
is stronger than this momentary affliction.

As long as I have breath in me,
I will sing Your song—
faith fanned into flame;
strength renewed;
as I run this race,
eyes fixed on You.[3]

1. John 15:16. 2. Matt. 13:44–46. 3. Heb. 12:1–2.

My bed has become an altar;
a temple of sacred memory.
In waking,
in dreaming,
You speak to me:
Guardian of My Soul.
Unraveler of Confusion.
Lifter of Sorrow.

I am a child,
clasped to its mother's breast;
cradled in the arms of love.

All that stands against me—
all that is godless,
graceless,
hell-bent—
will be swallowed by the grave;
a slow and painful death.

Good and Sustaining God;
the Ground of all my hope;
the Seat of all my desire—
I lift my hands;[4]
I lift my heart
to sing the glories of Your grace.
Your words are in my mouth—
a Living Language;
the native tongue of New Creation.

Your Truth will be revealed,
and evil will fall prostrate before it.

4. Ps. 63:4.

GOD WILL JUDGE

Father God,
in Your mercy,
deliver me from the fear of flesh—
from those who can kill body,
but not soul.[1]

Do not let them steal into the secret place;
into the shelter of Your presence;
where I am safe in Your shadow.[2]

Cover my eyes,
that I might not see the gathering of the godless;
the council of the cursed.

Cover my ears,
that I might not hear their plans of
destruction.
harm.
hopelessness.
ruin.

They delight in desecration;
boast in blasphemy;
suppressing Your knowledge
and Your judgment;[3]
turning from the truth;
wandering into myths;[4]
their delusion knows no bounds.

1. Matt. 10:28. 2. Ps. 91:1. 3. Rom. 1:18. 4. 2 Tim. 4:3–4.

I take comfort in this:
that You,
Maker of Heaven and Earth,
have a set a day of judgment;[5]
that all will stand before the Lamb[6]—
those clothed in Your righteousness
and those clothed in their own.

In that day,
You will put an end to wickedness;
You will strike down evil.
Death will lie in a grave of its own making,
a testament to all
of the fate that awaits the enemies of God.

I praise You, Lord,
for the miracle of grace;
that I am numbered among the redeemed—
Justified.
Sanctified.
Suffering with Christ,[7]
that I might bear a weight of glory beyond compare.[8]

5. Acts 17:31. 6. 2 Cor. 5:10. 7. Rom. 8:17. 8. 2 Cor. 4:17.

UNRESTRAINED

Lord God,
Your Presence
is my happy home;
Your Sanctuary
my temple of triumph.

See how the people of God
make pilgrimage to Your holy hill,
drawn by the heat of Your flame—
Your heart revealed to all.

We stagger forth with heavy need,
riddled with pain;
bent with sorrow.
You are faithful to
Hear us.
Hold us.
Mourn with us.
Mend us.

All who are called by You
know Your voice—
the quiet whisper of God, saying,
"Come away with me,
to Life Abundant,
filled to the brim,
spilling over;
for the Winter is over,
the Spring has come,[1]
and in My presence
there is fullness of joy."[2]

1. Song of Sol. 2:11–13. 2. Ps. 16:11.

Though sin plagues me,
You have broken its power;
reversed the curse
that held me in its sway.
You endured the cross;
the Lamb of God,
beaten and broken;
mocked and mutilated;
that my brokenness might be healed;[3]
my shame unwound;
my sorrow turned to joy in Your presence.[4]
You clothe us in garments of praise,[5]
welcoming us as children of God.

You are the worker of miracles;
Lord of the mighty and the meek,
who crafts
Concord from discord.
Light from shadow.
Hope from hopelessness.

Your words echo across the earth,
calling Your people home—
from every tribe,
nation,
tongue[6]—
that Your house may be full.

I would cross land and sea
to get to You;
to scale the hill of Your Sanctuary;
to know the shelter of Your presence.

Creation proclaims Your glory—
from snow-laden mountains
to the swirling depths of the sea;

3. Isa. 53:5. 4. Ps. 30:11. 5. Isa. 61:3. 6. Rev. 7:9.

flaring sun
to glimmering moon;
thundering storm
to waking dawn;
Your power and presence
are manifest;
Your faithfulness plain to see.

The earth quivers with Your Song:
Word-Shaped Wonder;
life unstoppable;
unending,
ever refreshed,
ever replenished;
river-rushing,
husk-bursting,
root-carving,
wheat-swaying,
rain-blessing,
sun-kissing,
star-glowing,
ocean-swelling,
canvas-stretching,
universe-expanding
Joy!

Creation is Your laughter,
unrestrained.

GOD OF ALL THINGS

God of all things,
may all things praise You.
May they join in holy harmony
with all that lives
and moves
and breathes
and is;
reality suspended on Your subatomic song;
the voice of God oscillating in every cell,
Binding.
Sustaining.
Inspiriting.

You are the King of Creation;
the Lord of snow-capped mountains
and desert wastes;
of rolling plains and roaring seas;
of
Laughter!
Bread!
Sex!
Sunrise!

You alone are worthy of
Adoration.
Praise.
Glory.

Are we not all walking images of God?[1]
Do not some, by their very existence,

1. Gen. 1:27.

praise You unaware?
And yet—
when their eyes are opened
to see You in Your glory,
even those who have cursed You
bend their knees.

Your creation is enough to warrant endless
Praise,
Wonder,
Awe.
But You are not just Creator,
Sustainer,
Upholder;
You have made Yourself Redeemer,
condescending to work miracles among us:
awesome displays of power,
bending the laws of
Nature,
Space,
Time;
and greater works still
done in quiet obscurity.

For all these things we thank You,
for You have not left us
unaware,
aloof,
ignorant—
but You have
Called us,
Gathered us,
Shepherded us—
that we might become children of God.[2]

2. John 1:12–13.

All history is Yours, Lord;
all thrones and dominions and powers.
The great civilizations of humanity will pass away,
while Your kingdom will have no end.[3]

May all who live know the riches of Your grace;[4]
the hope to which they are called;
the mercy of Your invitation.

Your way is not easy, Lord,
but it is Life.[5]
I've had my share of
afflictions,
confusions,
pains and heartaches.
I've often felt crushed beneath the weight of Your will,
desperate for some reprieve;
some end to this struggle.

But through it all,
ever so slowly,
You have shaped me;
molded me
into the likeness of Christ.[6]
Never have You left me.
Never have I been forsaken.[7]

I am waiting for the last stretch of road;
to crest that hill
and see the Promised Land I've been looking for all my life.

My heart overflows with gratitude
when I gather with Your saints,
proclaiming Your goodness;
resolving to walk in Your ways;

3. Luke 1:32–33. 4. Eph. 2:6–8. 5. Matt. 7:13–14. 6. Rom. 8:29.
7. Ps. 37:25.

to be single-minded in obedience.
For You were obedient even unto death.[8]

Were it not for that atoning blood
I could not stand before You;
were it not for Your resurrection breath
I could not suffer with such hope.

God forbid I should be silent about Your love!
Every rescued soul is a testimony to Your salvation;
every saved life
saved by the same saving grace.

All who look for You find You.
All who ask, seek, knock in humility,[9]
find that You were already there,
waiting.
You hear the cry of every human heart.
You, the God of all creation,
make Your dwelling with us;[10]
call us Your beloved.
Hallelujah!

8. Phil. 2:8. 9. Matt. 7:7–8. 10. John 1:14.

PRAISE, PRAISE, PRAISE

Father God,
praise wells up in me—
an uncontainable joy
at the thought of Your
kindness and care;
favor and fellowship;
the light of Your life
Upon me.
Around me.
Within me.

May I walk in that Light:
a picture of saving grace,
that others might taste and see
that You are good[1]
and worthy of all praise.

May they join in Your eternal song,
and with all created things
sing the glories of Your grace.[2]

You are sovereign over all—
all nations Your possession;
all peoples Your heritage;
the kingdoms of the world
dust on the scales[3]
to the God who inhabits eternity.

Dominion is Yours:
the rising and falling

1. Ps. 34:8. 2. Eph. 1:6. 3. Isa. 40:15.

of king and kingdom;
epoch and empire;
past and future
are in Your hands,
and You are faithful and true.[4]

Have You not given us all things?
The land pours out riches.
The sea bears fortunes.
Abundant provision!
Overflowing kindness!

Be praised, Lord—
from every corner of creation;
every tribe,
nation,
tongue.[5]

Be exalted!
Be lifted high!
With reverence
and holy awe,
may Your Name
be known in all the earth.[6]

4. Rev. 19:11. 5. Rev. 7:9. 6. 1 Kings 8:59–61.

PSALM 68

AT LAST!

God of all the earth,
You have said there will be a day—
not so very far away now—
when the Son of Man will come in power
to judge the living and the dead.[1]

Many will hide in terror
as He swings His sickle across the earth.[2]
All God-haters and Christ-mockers
will be trod in a winepress of wrath,[3]
to be made one with the nothingness they have
worshiped.

But Your children will feast
at the wedding supper of the Lamb,[4]
proclaiming Your great and glorious name:
Swallower of Death.[5]
Conqueror of Kingdoms.
Desire of Nations.[6]

We will sing the song of the redeemed;
an anthem of praise to You, our King,
for You did not leave us as orphans in our sin,[7]
but You came swiftly to deliver.
Jesus:
God Who Saves.

You are close to the brokenhearted;[8]
a friend to the downcast.

1. Acts 10:42; 2 Tim. 4:1; 1 Pet. 4:5. 2. Rev. 14:16. 3. Rev. 14:19.
4. Rev. 19:9. 5. Isa. 25:7. 6. Hag. 2:7. 7. John 14:18. 8. Ps. 34:18.

You dine with the weak,
the lonely,
the rejected.[9]

You are a jealous lover;[10]
a knight who storms castles
to rescue His beloved.
In Your house, there is a room
for every homeless heart.[11]

In Your presence, we flourish,
reflecting glory
like mirrors of the sun—
while the wicked fade into shadows.

Lead us, Lord,
as You led Your people in ages past:
with a cloud by day and fire by night;[12]
all nature at Your command.
You shepherded Your people,
carving a path through the desert;
none could stand before You.

At Your word,
the wilderness and the dry land were glad;
the desert rejoiced and blossomed.[13]
You drew rain from Heaven,
water from rock,
food from dust,
to provide for Your children:
a Faithful Father.
You gave them victory over their enemies,
guiding them to the Land of Promise.

---

9. Matt. 9:11; Mark 2:16; Luke 5:30. 10. Josh. 24:19; Exod. 20:5; 34:14;
Deut. 4:24. 11. John 14:2. 12. Exod. 13:21. 13. Isa. 35:1.

Now we,
like a people wandering in the desert,
await the promise of New Creation.
As the Israelites rejoiced at their victory—
joining in thunderous praise;
clothed in the plunder of battle;
a scorned and rejected people
arrayed like royalty—
we will rejoice at the last battle,
when evil is overthrown;
death disarmed;
and New Jerusalem is established
as the everlasting City of God.

Many look for the kingdom in the halls of power,
equating Your glory with pride and pomp;
great displays of military strength;
while You dwell with the humble and the lowly,[14]
choosing a cave over a castle;
a whisper over a wail;
repentant sinners
over pious pretenders.

You have hidden Your glory like treasure buried in a field,[15]
but it will not remain buried forever.
All that is hidden will be revealed.
All that is secret will come to light.[16]

If we could peek behind the veil;
if our eyes could be opened,
would we not see ranks of angel armies,
too many to number,
clothed in the power of God?
Would we not see You high and lifted up,
enthroned in Your cosmic temple,

14. Isa. 57:15. 15. Matt. 13:44. 16. Luke 8:17.

filling Heaven and earth,
as all proclaim
"Holy, holy, holy"?[17]

In Your mercy,
You invite all—
saints and sinners alike—
into the kingdom of God.
Your yoke is easy and Your burden is light.[18]

In faithfulness,
You bear our sorrows and our grief,[19]
strengthening us in the power of the Spirit,[20]
that we may enter Your rest,
ceasing from our works,
as You did on the seventh day.[21]

In the fullness of time,
Christ came among us:
conceived by Spirit,
born of woman,[22]
to suffer and die,
and shake free from death—
descending;
ascending[23]—
that all might be saved through Him
from the power of sin and the grave.[24]

You, who came in meekness,
will return in glory.[25]
The earth You have made will rejoice
at Your judgments;
the trees of the forest will sing for joy when
wickedness withers;[26]
darkness scatters;

17. Isa. 6:1–3. 18. Matt. 11:30. 19. Isa. 53:3. 20. 1 Cor. 12:9–10. 21. Heb.
4:9–11. 22. Gal. 4:4. 23. Eph. 4:8–10. 24. Rom. 6:9–11. 25. Mark 13:26.
26. 1 Chron. 16:33.

bondage ceases.
All creation will cry out,
"At last! At last!"[27]

A great multitude will follow You
from every tribe and nation:[28]
the cheerful citizens of New Creation.
With joyous songs they will proclaim,
"Hallelujah!
All things are made new!"[29]

In that day,
the streets of New Jerusalem
will be filled with the sound of laughter;
of music and song.[30]
There will be no temple;
no sun or moon;
for You will be our light.[31]
You will gather Your children about You,
and they will weep no more.[32]

The glory of the Lord will be known throughout the earth.
Rulers will bring their tributes.
Far-flung nations will come
to pay their allegiance to the One True King.

The doors of Your City will never be shut,[33]
and the leaves of the tree of life
will bring healing to those who freely come.[34]
But the insolent,
the proud,
the bloodthirsty,
will be blotted out;
forgotten;
many who are first will be last.

27. Rom. 8:21. 28. Rev. 7:9; 19:1. 29. Rev. 21:5. 30. Jer. 31:4.
31. Rev. 21:22–23. 32. Rev. 21:4. 33. Rev. 21:24–26. 34. Rev. 22:2.

The earth will be filled with the knowledge of Your salvation
as the waters cover the sea.[35]
The nations will break out in song,
turning their hearts to You:
Maker of all things;
the great and glorious God
who condescended to dwell among us.
The Word Made Flesh.[36]

Creation testifies to Your power and goodness.
Your rains fall on the just and the unjust.[37]
Your desire is that all would be saved[38]—
every knee bow,
every tongue confess,[39]
all rebels lay down their arms
and enter Your joy.[40]

May it be so, Lord!
Amen.

35. Hab. 2:14. 36. John 1:14. 37. Matt. 5:45. 38. Isa. 45:22; 1 Tim. 2:4. 39. Isa. 45:23; Phil. 2:10–11. 40. Matt. 25:21.

THE NAME THAT SAVES

Lord Jesus,
I am lost on a raging sea.
The waters churn about me,
my boat filling up—
a slow, sinking death.

With fear
and little faith[1]
I cry out to You:
the Name That Saves.

Sometimes the darkness is so heavy,
the pain so great,
that all light is blotted out;
the heavens painted black;
and I am lost in the gloom—
a forgotten thing,
plunging into the void.

Do You not hear me?
Do You not see?
Must these prayers go unanswered forever?
My strength wastes away.

While You are silent,
the darkness speaks:
voices murmuring in the night;
a gathering choir of curses
surrounding me,
assaulting me,
weaving a web of shame around me.

1. Luke 12:28.

I refuse to believe that my suffering
is the result of Your judgment.
Not that I am not without sin—
far from it—
but You have been faithful to forgive,
removing my transgressions;
casting them behind Your back.

This cannot be the end of my story, Lord.
For what would that say to a watching world?
I hold out hope that You will bring some good from this.

May I remember that
there is no greater honor
than to share in Your sufferings;[2]
to be pitied for my passion;
disdained for my devotion;
mocked for my mercy.

May my life be pleasing in Your sight, Lord;[3]
and in Your time may You redeem it.

For the darkness threatens to consume me;
to utterly devour me;
to wrench me from the land of the living.

Show Yourself, Lord.[4]
If You are for me,
save me!
If You love me,
deliver me!
Do not be silent—
speak!
Do not be distant—
press in!

2. 1 Pet. 4:13. 3. Ps. 19:14. 4. 2 Sam. 22:26.

Twist into good
what the Enemy meant for evil.[5]

Nothing is hidden from Your sight.[6]
You see the sin that afflicts me;
the pride that binds me;
all trespasses,
within and without:
the full extent of my brokenness.

I find no comfort in friends;
no peace in companionship—
only bloodless counsel;
empty wisdom.

May the lies of the wicked return to them;
their curses undo them.
May they lose their language,
their bite;
stumbling in their sayings;
babbling in their prophecies.
May the evil they have sown
come back to haunt them;
Your judgment fall heavy upon them.

Such is the fate of those who oppose You;
who attack the children of Your covenant.
They are banished from the land of the living,
cast into the Weeping Place.

My soul is in Your hands, Lord.
I carry in my body
Your death,
that Your life
may be manifested in me.[7]

5. Gen. 50:20. 6. Heb. 4:13. 6. 2 Cor. 4:8–12.

May praise well up in my soul;
defiant thanks
to lift the weary spirit:
a pleasing sacrifice to You;
a witness to all
that You give beauty for ashes;
the oil of joy for mourning.[7]

You are close to the poor in spirit;
a friend to captives;
the lifter of the heavy-hearted.

Be praised
by these violent waters;
for were they not made by You,
and all that is in them?
All creatures of the deep—
dolphins, cerulean blue;
narwhals, tusked and mottled grey;
countless unseen marvels
teeming,
swarming
in praise.

I will sing—
though the sea roars about me
and my boat reels and rocks beneath me—
for You will see me through this tempest.
I will stand again on solid ground,
safe in the Land of Your Promise.
Amen.

7. Isa. 61:3.

LORD OVER DEATH
AND DARKNESS

Father,
Your ways are slow and steady,
unhurried by our busyness;
kairos to our *chronos*.
But today, I can't afford to wait.
I need You now!
Let Your mercy be swift;
Your rescue unhindered.

The Enemy has me cornered,
pleased to exploit my weakness;
twisting his thorn into my flesh.

Grant me strength, Lord.

Can You not scatter these dark spirits
with the sound of a thundering army,
or twist their devil tongues to confusion?

For You,
Lord of light and beauty,
are Lord over death and darkness as well—
all evil prostrate at Your feet;
powerless in Your presence.
Send these taunting voices back to the depths of the earth
where they belong.

I have sung many songs in the house of God
with joy in my heart;
strength in my bones;
joining with all the redeemed
to proclaim Your goodness and faithfulness.

But today, I am broken;
my faith a withered vine.
Have mercy upon me, Lord,
for You are my only hope
in life and death;
I have no good apart from You.[1]
Come swiftly to my aid!
Lift me from this darkness.

1. Ps. 16:2.

ALWAYS AN EDEN

There is always an Eden—
a place of solace,
away from noise and clamor;
from shame that pursues me.

In love,
You lead;
in faithfulness,
You listen;
as we walk together
in the cool of the day[1]—
the ground firm beneath my feet;
my soul secure in Your presence.

In that place,
I have no fear of danger
from encroaching darkness—
for You are with me.
My Strength.
My Shield.

Looking back,
I see that my life
is a picture of Your providence.
From the shadow of the womb,
You guided my growth in grace.
When I was young,
Your Spirit taught me courage.
Never was I alone;
never was I unloved.

1. Gen. 3:8.

Praise leads me into Your presence again—
to our meeting place;
our table of communion.
Save me from the love of lesser gods;
the worship of the unworthy.
My glory is You!

I have known suffocating rejection;
the soul-sickness that comes with it:
the mounting panic;
tightness of chest;
but You have been breath to me—
lung-swelling oxygen
in thin air.

Days pass into years;
years pass into memory.
I age,
slowed by labor;
wearied by struggle.
When time grows short,
may I lean upon Your strength
and stagger toward glory.

I am cursed for Your name's sake;
called coward for trusting You;
fool for following You.
Darkness plots my downfall,
confident in Your distance
and indifference.

Draw near, Lord!
Prove Yourself to be
a present help in trouble;[2]
the Great High Priest of Heaven.[3]

2. Ps. 46:1. 3. Heb. 4:14.

Evil cannot stand before You.
Wickedness cannot abide Your glory.
All godless things must bow.

As for me,
I will hold to Your promises;
stand on Your faithfulness;
exalting You with thankful praise—
proclaiming Your mercy;
declaring Your goodness;
sharing the riches
of the mystery of Christ,
the hope of glory[4]—
for You alone are
Holy.
Worthy.
True.

In my younger years,
I sat at Your feet,
an eager learner.
And now,
You still have much to teach me.

Age takes us all.
One day, we are young;
then we are old.
Time slips from our hands.

Be near to me
when my days near their end.
For I have unfinished business
in this land of passing things:
to tell of the Most High God,
who moved Heaven and earth

4. Col. 1:27; 2:2.

to be near those He loved.
May the Story be told, Lord,
again and again,
generation to generation,
while time tarries.

It echoes
from every corner of creation;
the Highest Heaven
could not contain You![5]
Your love is relentless.
Your mercy, endless.[6]

Though I have wandered into dangerous lands,
where evil surrounds;
trouble follows;
have had my share of sorrows,
struggles,
afflictions—
You have been faithful to
Find me.
Lift me.
Resurrect me.

I am revived by Your Spirit.
Enlivened by Your Love.
Empowered by Your Strength.

God forbid these instruments
should collect dust.
I will make a joyful noise, Lord,
for You are my
Lyric,
Melody,
Rhythm,

5. 1 Kings 8:27; 2 Chron. 6:18. 6. Lam. 3:22.

Rhyme—
the anthem of my heart;
the One who
Saved me.
Delivered me.
Embraced me!

For the powers of darkness
will be broken;
evil undone.
The earth will know peace again,
and You will make Your home with us
forever.

A PRAYER FOR THOSE IN POWER

Father,
may Your will be done by all those in power.
In Your grace, open their minds to wisdom;
their hearts to justice;
their souls to mercy.
May they lead with love,
seeking Your pleasure
over riches
or honor
or the approval of others.

If they seek Your face,
favor will follow—
blessing upon blessing;
every need met by Your faithfulness.

Give them a heart for the downhearted;
the crushed in spirit;
the lonely and forgotten.
Show them how to walk in Your ways—
seeking justice for the weak;
befriending the friendless.[1]

In the din of voices,
may they hear Yours above all,
and know the wisdom
bought by fear of You.
Let them not depart from it;

1. Ps. 82:3.

keep them rooted in truth:
river trees in good soil,[2]
enduring for generations.

A godly leader seeks the good of the people;
becomes a conduit for Your grace.
Where You are glorified,
the hungry are fed;
the guilty pardoned;
the enslaved freed.

May Your kingdom be established in the earth!
We see it in fleeting glimpse and shadow:
signs of the eternal rest to come.

In this age of darkness,
may righteous rulers abound,
preparing the way for Your eternal rule.
Let those in peaceful power
continually expand their boundaries,
carrying the cup of mercy to the ends of the earth—
from north to south,
east to west.

When Your kingdom comes,
our games of conquest will come to an end.
All knees will bend[3]—
all crowns relinquished;
thrones abandoned.
You,
and You alone,
will reign.

Is it too much, Lord,
to ask for justice before that day?

2. Ps. 1:3. 3. Phil. 2:9–11.

For leaders who seek Your will above all?
Who value righteousness over reputation?
Mercy over material things?
Who seek the liberation of the oppressed?
The nourishment of the hungry?
The rescue of the captive?

The halls of power are filled with wickedness.
Raise up the righteous to drive them out,
and so establish a colony of Your coming kingdom.

Bless them with health;
honor;
resources;
may the prayers of the saints give them strength.
In all that they do,
may they flourish—
cup filled to overflowing;[4]
all the needs of the people met;
more than we could ask or imagine.
Give us a glimpse of Your New Creation—
a picture of peace;
of true justice;
of this violent world at rest at last.

If we are to celebrate the kingdoms of earth,
let us celebrate those that have looked to You.
May we remember the godly
over the great;
the magnanimous
over the mighty.

For You are the true King—
the God who rules and reigns over all.

4. Ps. 23:5.

You alone are worthy of
Praise.
Honor.
Adoration.

For this fractured earth will one day
be covered with glory
as the waters cover the sea.[5]
Come, Lord Jesus!
Amen.

5. Hab. 2:14.

THIS PLACE WE MEET

Lord,
You are good to those who wrestle with You;
who are bound to Your strength;
wed to Your working;
trained by Your touch;
who keep their hearts clean
as they struggle through life.

God knows I have danced with death,
skirting the edge of the cliff;
the chasmic dark below me.

I have lusted after wealth and power,
coveting the gain of the godless;
my bones sick with envy.

They live in blissful ignorance,
satisfied with passing pleasures;
accumulating more and more;
free from the burden of righteousness;
the thorn of temptation.[1]
They don't know trouble like I do, Lord.
They are unacquainted with suffering,
with grief—
the clash of flesh and spirit.

They adorn themselves in comforting lies—
a threaded cloak of pride;
a garment soaked in blood;
they know not what violence they breed.

1. 2 Cor. 12:7.

They are engorged with lust;
their souls deformed;
their minds defiled.
They sneer at the poor;
ridicule the righteous.

They run their mouths,
prattling on and on—
a steady stream of careless curses;
contempt for any truth beyond themselves.
They multiply in number;
a raucous throng hastening into the grave.

They talk of You as if You're not even there—
as if You are distant,
deaf,
dead,
and the world is better off without You.

They rest in peace,
wanting for nothing,
their borders ever expanding.

I have set my hope on You, Lord.
I have been steadfast,
whole-hearted,
worshiping in spirit and truth[2]—
meditating on Your goodness;
feeding on Your Word;
my hands clean from violence.

But sometimes it feels like I get nothing
for my effort;
no reward for my faithfulness;
only trouble upon trouble,
struggle upon struggle.

2. John 4:24.

It feels as if You've forgotten me
I wake to pain in the morning
and suffer madness through the day.

But then I come into Your presence
and worship before You—
rejoicing in Your goodness,
Your kindness,
Your love—
and the darkness is revealed to me;
the shadows are illuminated.
And I see
with startling clarity
the truth that had escaped me:

It is the wicked who stumble;
the godless who are destined to fall.
My feet slipped for a moment,
but theirs will fall from the heights of their arrogance;
they will plunge headfirst into the void,
dragged down by the devils they have worshiped.

My heart has been so heavy, Lord;
my mind so dense with confusion;
like a rock weighed down in water,
sunk to the lowest place.

In my darkest moments,
I have felt less than human—
a dim reflection of my former self.

But even in my madness,
You were with me.
When I stumbled blind,
You were my sight.
I cannot escape You.

I have searched the world
and have found no lasting hope;
no abiding joy
outside Your presence.

In crippling weakness,
You are my strength.
When I draw my final breath,
You will breathe new life into me.
I will look upon You
in all Your glory,
and the old things will be forgotten.

For only that which has died
and been reborn
will live forever.
All that stands against You—
all pride,
evil,
violence,
villainy—
is destined to die,
never to rise again.

As for me,
I walk on holy ground—
beholding Your beauty;
resting in Your kindness;
sheltering in Your presence.

May my life be a picture of grace
to a hurting world—
a living sacrifice;
a testament to Your salvation.

REMEMBER US

Father,
sometimes it feels as if You have forgotten us—
that our sins are so great;
our transgressions so deep;
that no mercy is left in Your heart—
that we have exhausted Your grace
and are left only with judgment.

Were we not bought with Your blood?
Raised to new life?
Can Your free gift be revoked?
Reversed?
Are we not Yours forever?
Members of the household of God—
the place where You dwell?

And yet,
wolves have crept into the sheepfold.
Your Bride has been lured by lies—
a slow seduction;
incremental compromise—
Your sanctuary has become a den of robbers.[1]
We are a house divided.
A kingdom corrupted.

Brick by brick,
we have been deconstructed,
dismantled,
destroyed.
We are a ruin—

1. Matt. 21:13.

a forgotten place,
looted by enemies;
haunted by the dead—
a sobering reminder
of all that stands in the way
of the world.

The power of Your Spirit
is a distant memory—
a faint recollection
of a time when we walked in
vision,
insight,
revelation.

Is there hope for us yet?
Can You draw us from this darkness?
Deliver us from this oppression?
When will we be Your Joyous Bride again?
When will we be made ready
for the wedding feast?

May the hand of Your judgment
fall heavy upon all that stands against You
and the children of Your covenant.

For You are King of all the earth—
Author and Perfecter of Salvation;[2]
Mighty in power;
Awesome in glory;
Sea-Splitter,
Dragon-Tamer,
River-Maker,
Desert-Carver.
All creation is Yours—

2. Heb. 12:1–2.

earth and sun,
moon and stars,
bird and beast;
the frost of Winter;
the blossom of Spring—
all exists for Your glory,
Your fame,
Your pleasure.

Remember us, Lord;
remember who we are to You,
and what curses are leveled against us.
Like a dog in the street,
we are battered,
beaten,
left for dead.

Remember us, Lord;
remember the mercy of Your cross
and the promise of a world made new.
For evil spreads its fingers around the earth,
bringing unspeakable pain;
unfathomable violence—
for how long?

How long will this deep darkness last?
How long will the innocent suffer before You act?
Restore us, Lord!
Pour out Your Spirit upon us!
May our sons and daughters prophesy;
our old dream again;
our young see visions![3]

May these ruins be rebuilt,
brick by brick.[4]

3. Joel 2:28. 4. Isa. 58:12.

May Your bride adorn herself
in holiness again,
that we might be presented to You in splendor.[5]
For You have loved us from before the foundation of the world,[6]
and You will see us safely home.

5. Eph. 5:27. 6. Eph. 1:4–6.

THE TIMES
OF YOUR KNOWING

Lord God,
my heart overflows with praise—
like a house on holiday:
a joyful gathering
of story and song—
holy chatter;
cheerful clamor;
recollecting mercy.

For You have shaken the heavens and the earth,[1]
stooping to enter human history—
suffering,
dying,
rising—
to rescue Your beloved.
Everywhere I look, the Story is told:
creation rehearsing death and resurrection
until the end.

For darkness will not have the final word.
You, who came in meekness,
will return in majesty,
the time of harvest
known by You alone,
to bless or curse
the wheat and weed.[2]

1. Hag. 2:6. 2. Matt. 13:30.

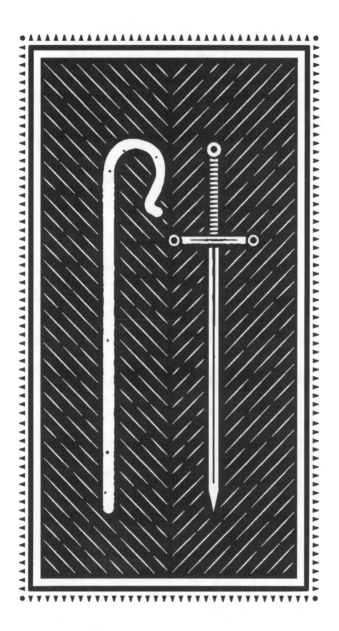

You hold eternity in Your hands—
all that was,
that is,
that ever will be—
safe in Your keeping.

You offer peace to Your enemies
in exchange for the surrender of the will.
You draw near to the humble;
You resist the proud.[3]

What a
shaking,
quaking,
faking lot we are—
lured by lust;
panting for power.

We place our hopes in
lowercase gods.
short-term saviors.
fleeting promises.

We have strayed from You,
looking for truth where it can't be found;
searching for water in empty wells.

You set before us life and death:
Your will,
or ours,
be done[4]—
Light or darkness.
Peace or peril.
Glory or grave.

3. James 4:6. 4. Matt. 26:39–44.

Give me the strength to choose You, Lord,
each day a fresh start:
new mercies to discover;
new songs to sing
as I limp on,
hip-stolen and surrendered—
one who has striven with God and mortals,
and lived to tell the tale.[5]

In Your time,
You will return to us—
to vanquish evil;
destroy death;
establish Your everlasting kingdom.
We will walk in Your light,
lacking nothing;
healed at last.

Lord,
Your presence is life to me:[6]
joy of my heart;
strength of my soul.
Amen.

5. Gen. 32:28. 6. Ps. 16:11.

✵ ACKNOWLEDGMENTS ✵

This book has been several years in the making, and there are many people to thank. We owe a great debt of gratitude to Carolyn Weber, who encouraged this work from the very beginning. In all likelihood it would have remained a mere poetic exercise if not for her enthusiasm and support. Many heartfelt thanks to Bob Hosack and the entire team at Brazos for catching the vision for a collection of "free-verse prayer renderings." To all the friends and family members who reviewed and prayed these prayers with us along the way, we are grateful. Finally, a special thanks to our wives, Patti and Anita, and our children for their ongoing love and support.